PRAISE FOR
ROADCUTS THROUGH THE HEART

"I loved Roadcuts Through the Heart. This memoir of a white southern boy growing into manhood as he comes to grips with sex and love, race and power while, at the same time, wrestling with his upbringing in a deeply troubled family, rings almost too poignantly true. Moving back and forth over time, Weddell takes us on a journey from his childhood in sleepy, segregated Athens, Georgia in the years before it became an alternative music and culture scene to his eye-opening experiences at Columbia University where he was caught up in the uprising of 1968. And he does so eloquently, humbly, and with the unmistakable sting of wisdom that is hard-won."

—Jacquelyn Dowd Hall, retired history professor
University of North Carolina at Chapel Hill

Roadcuts through the Heart

Roadcuts through the Heart

A Georgia Memoir

Deeds Publishing | Athens

Published by Deeds Publishing in Athens, GA
www.deedspublishing.com

Printed in The United States of America

ISBN 978-1-950794-50-8

Books are available in quantity for promotional or premium use. For information, email info@deedspublishing.com.

First Edition, 2021

10 9 8 7 6 5 4 3 2 1

Contents

For Bertie

Nonetheless, truth was conspiring to assemble itself before me. Call it fate, or grace, or pure shithouse chance.

— Mary Karr, *The Liars' Club*

1. Slope Stakes

Etiquette

It started so innocently.

A promising warm Saturday morning in '55 Georgia, cartoons over, and I was a boy on a mission. My sister Caroline had spent the night at a friend's house, so Mom had OK'd a first by-myself bike-trip to the neighborhood commercial area, Five Points.

It couldn't have been an easy call for Mom. Caroline liked to watch out for me, did what she was told, didn't crash as much as I did, and always used her kickstand.

Just looking at the two bikes you could see the difference.

Stay on the sidewalk, Jimmy. I know you wouldn't disappoint me, Mom guilted. And I was off.

My destination was Hodgson's Drugs, our everything store. It had a soda-fountain along one wall (not a self-serve machine, but a full-service, sit-down place with counter stools, ice cream, milk shakes, fountain drinks, and snacks; the counter where we were in the midst of learning the delight found in adding cherry syrup to our cokes); a lending library in the back corner (five cents per book per week); the pharmacy along the back wall (which also served as a little post office); several aisles of cold remedies, tooth brushes and paste, first aid stuff, enema bags, canes and crutches; a few toys; model airplane, ship, and car kits; and a wooden magazine display. But the most important items for me were the spinning metal comic book racks, which sat right down front, almost in front of the wide glass double doors.

Standing at those racks without paying, I read a lot of comic books. It didn't seem quite right, but I couldn't resist the free reading. Doing that, two days before, I had seen a twenty-five cent *Lone Ranger* book which captured my heart. Comic books were regularly merely a dime, but this was a thick special issue. It had the whole Lone Ranger legend—how his family was wiped out in a wagon-train massacre, why he had the silver bullets, where they came from—plus lots of new stories. Twenty-five cents was a lot of money, but I was going to own Lone Ranger myself.

So there I was, safely down at Hodgson's about to go in the door, my bike up on its stand for a change, when a lady came up behind me. I stopped as I was taught and opened the door for her. She hesitated a moment but walked through, thanking me over her shoulder.

I followed her in, both of us breathing in the air conditioning with relief, and every pair of eyeballs in the store was staring at us. The soda-jerk, the guy who ran the fountain counter, especially. His jaw was unhinged and his neck recovering from whiplash.

Judging from the way he and Hodgson's customers were fixed on us, Mom and Dad's lessons about etiquette had neglected something. Apparently, the rule about opening doors for ladies applied to White people only.

The Trap

Probably two years later, and a little before Mom's quitting time, I came out of the Athens YMCA building, my second home, by myself. This was unusual, since normally at five o'clock—after school, when our time at the Y was up—I was part of a pack of giggling, yelling, pushing, shoving, nine-and-ten-year-old White boys, still full of energy though we'd spent over two hours fiercely contesting whatever sport was in season.

We ended with a swim before changing back into our school clothes, and spilled out of the side-door into a tiny, sandy playground with mon-key-bars and a jungle-gym—the old, vaguely dome-shaped gray metal kind—searching for our moms or carpools.

If neither was in sight we'd mess around in the little playground, and, in one of those brief windows of opportunity, I had once jumped from the jungle-gym and come oh-so-close to catching my intended target, the near top rail of the monkey-bars. My resulting chin-first impact with the sandy dirt below drove my buck teeth right through my lower lip, and I hardly cried at all. At least that's what I told myself.

But this day was different. No basement door exit for me. I ran up the stairs inside the building, trotted purposefully across the lobby past the offices and meeting rooms on what the grown-ups probably thought was the main floor (we kids thought the basement with the sports stuff, pool, showers, and lockers was the main floor), and went out the formal front doors.

I was supposed to go by myself over to Mom's new workplace, across the sometimes frantic four-lane street which ran in front of the Y, and a block further toward the river. Turning in at the entrance to the Univer-sity of Georgia's old campus.

Something bothered me. The sky was wrong. It was barely the blue side of black, a color too dark for twilight.

These days I told everyone I was fine if they asked how I was doing. But I wasn't. I was only covering, pretending Mom wasn't falling apart. And pretending somewhere deep I wasn't terrified something worse was going to happen to me, Caroline, and our older, not-quite-like-every-one-else's sister Mary Win.

Right then I was scared a disaster was waiting for me at the office where Mom was trying to work as a secretary. At home she wasn't acting like everything was hunky-dory.

The sky wasn't helping my mood.

I made my way to the corner, crossed the not-pedestrian-friendly street, and walked beside the intimidating, spear-like pickets in the university's fence until I came to the wrought-iron arch and entered the campus.

The old Academic Building was easy to recognize, with its four columns and fancy outside staircases visible behind them. Mom's office was on the second floor off the left-hand staircase. I knew this, but still breathed easier once I found it.

Then I saw Mom. Head down on a desk. Sobbing under a pool of yellow light from her desk lamp. The tears had slacked off some since she'd gotten the job, the job that was supposed to pull the family back together, to solve everything—both Mom's crying jags and our money woes.

Dad hadn't left us much to live on when he died, unless we sold the house. Her crying at her new office—alone in the dark with only the sick yellow light from the goose-neck—made me feel like an ocean wave had knocked me down and was dragging me out.

I tried to think of what to say. To think of what would make her stop the flow. But I couldn't.

When she saw me she started weeping harder. I went over to her and put my scrawny nine-year-old arms around her and I could feel her gathering her breath, trying to stop, but she'd get a little way down the drier road and start up again. I was so helpless I couldn't fight back my own tears.

We needed to go home. We needed to get out of this place. But Mom had to stop blubbering. *Please Mom, please stop crying.* I didn't tell her I needed her to stop leaking, that I couldn't do this by myself.

It'll be alright Mom. You'll be OK. Nothing. *We'll be OK.* But I was trying as hard to convince myself as I was her. *Snuifufuf... snuffnn, snuuffhnn,* she sniffed, trying to suck back her tears through her nose.

After forever, she found her breath and pulled her head up and glanced at me. *I... I... I'm su... su... sorry.* She started to cry again when she did that, but managed somehow to stuff it back down. Another forever passed, she worked out some words between hiccups. *It'll be alright*, she whispered. *It'll be alright.*

I wanted so much to believe her, but I couldn't. I could only feel an overwhelming desperation to get out of there with her. I had to be home. No matter if she was still crying, home offered a security I could believe more than I could believe her.

She told me more than I wanted to know. She'd been fired. This job which was supposed to be our lifeline was a trap. She couldn't stop the waterfall even at work. They'd let her go.

Getting and then in no time losing a job was worse than not getting one. Now we were hopeless.

She told me this on the way home. The sky grew ever darker, clearly threatening, and the customarily friendly trees were suddenly leafless and black. I hated this. I wanted to be home with Caroline and Mary Win. I wanted Dad to be alive again. I wanted Mom to be herself. And I wanted to feel safe.

She Wasn't Always Like That

I got to ride in the wagon with the pigs!

Mom, with a rare wistful smile, was retelling her early 1900s excitement at the move from Lansing, Michigan to a tiny farm 120 miles away, outside the much smaller Big Rapids. No teenage angst for her.

She loved the pig ride. Named every one of them.

Isabel and Dorothy for my sisters. Clarence and CP for their boyfriends.

After they settled in at the farm, the kids from her part of the county were accepting, she made friends, and claimed to have loved the six-mile round trip walk to the one-room VanGilder School.

Learning came easy, her Palmer Method penmanship was like

engraving, and she outshone the farm boys in memorizing and reciting the breeds of sheep of Michigan — *Middle Wool: Southdowns; Shropshires; Hampshires; Oxfords; Dorsets; Cheviots; Suffolks; Tunis. Long Wool: Cotswold; Leicester; Lincoln; Romney Marsh; Wensleydale; Devon Long Wool. Fine Wool: American Merino A; American Merino B; American Merino C; Rambouillet.*

This she delighted in reciting to anyone who cared to ask and many who didn't.

She and her folks returned to Lansing her senior year. Money and farming got tight in the country. Again, no stress for Winifred, Win to her friends, my mom. Lansing, only a middling city in Michigan, was nonetheless big enough to have a taste of the Roaring Twenties about it. Prohibition, raids on stills, speakeasies, women smoking, women clubbing unchaperoned. Heady times to be starting on your own.

After high school graduation, Mom went to business school, landed a good job, advanced from department secretary to personal secretary for the Michigan State president, bought a car — her first, a new Ford — and drove it with verve. (Although her verve included a nasty clutch-riding tendency never to be changed.)

It would be easy, but wrong, to picture her on the edges of the flapper scene. Sitting in a dim club with a flask in her garter, bobbed hair, cloche hat, slinky dress, and made-up face. Listening to hot music. Dancing, and showing a lot of leg.

She had the attitude, her earned money, the face, the thin build, the clothes sense, the people-person personality. Only it wouldn't have happened. She wouldn't go for the booze, the cigarettes, or the taste in music. Her Methodist, teetotaler, anti-Demon Rum sentiments ran deep, as did her preference for church music.

The dancing would have tempted her. But bowling was more her choice, and where she and Don, my Dad, had their first date.

It happened this way, Caroline said. *Mom would tease people. Like you*

6

do. She met this good-looking — the most handsome man she'd ever seen, Mom said — grad student at the president's office. He asked her out. She had plans with friends, but (ha, ha!) he could show up if he wanted to.

He showed up. At a bowling alley of course. Surprising everyone, and he and she were smitten.

I Wasn't Always Like That Either

John L's birthday parties were events of wonder. Starting in first grade. His mother would come to school with cake, ice cream held cold by dry ice, punch, little Confederate flags for us to wear and wave around, and music to which she marched us around, serenading John. To my mind it was the highlight of the school year.

In kindergarten she took us all — boys, girls, both classrooms — to the Athens Country Club. By the time we got to the edge of town we were wound so tight we exploded out of the cars like shook-up Coke from a bottle.

I raced ahead of the swarm, over the too-green grass, down the hill, towards the clubhouse. The hill flattened down faster than my little legs could shorten up, and every one of my schoolmates landed on top of me.

That running, running only for the feel of it — the wind, the heart — was worth the trip to the E.R. The sling for the cracked wrist made up for missing the ice cream.

Driving with Dad

The family drove a lot when I was little. Mom and Dad up front. Me and my sisters Caroline and Mary Win in the back seat of a huge '48 Oldsmobile. I was the baby of the bunch, born in '47. Caroline was born in '45, three months after World War II ended. Mary Win was much older, a Depression Era baby, arriving with difficulty in 1934, two years past Mom and Dad's marriage.

Dad's routes took us over Georgia. Out to Lexington in the next county where Dad's tree farm was; down to Savannah where the beach, the fort, the horseflies, and the Spanish moss and pulp mills were; up to Dahlonega where the gold rush began and you ate family-style at the Smith House or jumped into the teeth-chattering-cold lake at 4-H Camp Wahsega if you were brave enough; on south to Eatonton—Uncle Remus's home and where the Woodland Indians' big Rock Eagle was merely a mound until you climbed the White man's tower and looked down; out to Winterville to visit the chicken-farming Harrolds in the country and admire their architect-designed home with the back porch in the center of the house; and over to big city Atlanta, seventy-two miles on a wandering two-lane road, passing by the hauntingly abandoned Confederate carving on Stone Mountain.

Sometimes we'd stop, and Dad, a professional forester, would get out and explore a stand of pines. I never knew what caught his eye in those trees, but I was transfixed by the roadcuts along the highway. They were eroded red clay slopes, steep slopes which never healed. The mighty kudzu plant itself couldn't hold them. Kudzu which could conquer everything else moving slowly or not at all—trees, power lines, houses, windmills, barns, dead cars, dead tractors, maybe small sleeping boys. Kudzu brought over from Japan to stop this fissuring and sliding was powerless against the will of the clay to move with the rain.

I loved focusing down onto and into the crevices in those roadcuts and thinking about what an ant or smaller creature might see in the scratchy texture of the clay. I saw those cracks as a land of rugged ridges and valleys with scattered plateaus and tabletops where pieces of mica and silica sheltered bits of clay from the power carried in small drops of water. I saw caves and box canyons, dry riverbeds and earthen dams, a world torn and scarred. Years later, when I first saw the Dakota Badlands and Eastern Washington Scablands, I knew they were somehow familiar.

What the Children Saw

Leaning over the back of the big front seat, looking beyond the grown-ups' heads out through the windshield, little bellies snugged tight to the seat-back, against the worn cloth-covered rope whose purpose was opaque. Did Dad's hand reach snake-like over to Mom's knee and give it a squeeze?

Oh, Don, not in front of the children!

What did a giggle and a smile have to do with those words?

2. Roadsides

Palm Reading

It was a quiet time in the house. Mom and my sisters were downtown and Beulah Mae and I were alone. I was still in short pants and wandered around following her, watching her work. She made everything seem easy. Doing the dishes, making the beds, sweeping the front porch. Sometimes humming nice tunes. She got to the dusting part, and I knew it would take some time. Mom had a lot of fragile keepsakes on shelves and table tops.

We were in the living room, the room a shade of robin's-egg-blue which I lived with uneasily. Now I would say it was a tint too cool. When I was four I didn't have the concepts or the words, only the disquiet. Mom loved the color. Kept it for years. It was elegant, I'll give it that.

Dad had a corner of the room which everyone recognized as his. A wing-backed easy chair in blue brocade with a matching footstool so he could settle in and read the newspaper when he got home. Taking off his black shoes and putting his white socked feet up on the stool. Turning on the four-way floor lamp to get the right light. And tuning in the new shelf-model Bakelite radio softly so he could both read and listen. The corner was his homecoming place.

And where Beulah Mae was dusting. The built-in bookcase beside his chair. Dusting the long blue china box full of old coins, a watch chain with some fobs, a paper clip or two, and his toenail clipper. The box had gilt trim on it, but the top was broken in two pieces, and nobody ever fixed it.

11

Beulah Mae started dusting at the top of the bookcase, standing on the little footstool she pulled over from Mom's pink rocker. Using a short-handled turkey-feather duster which had been around my whole short life she carefully fluffed the knick-knacks on the top shelf. Next she was down off the stool dusting the books and the radio. I never saw the dust. But it must have been there.

I was thinking about asking Beulah Mae something.

We didn't talk much, but it was an easy silence. I waited till she put the last keepsake down and I asked her, *Beulah Mae, how come the palms of your hands are white and the top sides brown?*

This was something I wanted to know. It seemed so different. My hands were much the same, one side or the other, but hers were not. One side of hers was this pretty brown color and the other side was a weathered pink earthworm shade. Why was that?

I thought there'd be a simple answer, but Beulah Mae only stared at me and left the room. I did not understand. Mom almost always had something to say, whether it made sense to me or not, or was so sideways I had to guess what she meant.

Beulah Mae's silence and walking out was saddening and less understandable than anything Mom had ever said. I must have done something wrong.

Athens, Georgia 1955

Athens remains beautiful. Especially the older parts, though it's grown three times its former size. In my day its graciousness provided a contrast to the hardscrabble country nearby. The rough setting is gone now, but the gem remains. Well-mannered, colonnaded, pre-Civil War mansions continue to distinguish its main streets. Dogwoods pink and white persist, keeping their pact with my childhood streets.

Our house stands, and the old yard stays filled with tall branching water oaks. Although the scuppernong arbor is gone, neighbors' magnolias provide climbing opportunities for a new generation of kids, as well as huge but delicate blossoms to grace their moms' tables.

Athens is a university town, and, in the '50s and '60s, to those of us inside the White, middle-class system, faculty and staff were like an extended family. Old-school collegiality was in flower and the grown-ups were easily showing the kids how to *work and play well with others* in higher education. Through a meshwork of shared passions—gardening, hunting, fishing, football, sewing, religion, music, gossip—and social clubs, civic clubs, service clubs, and religious organizations, they saw each other more often and in more different lights than common in current academic life. The gap between administrators and professors was small, and research, publication, and impact factor had not gained ascendancy over teaching.

When I was growing up, kids were allowed, and encouraged, to come with their parents to the president's reception on the grounds of the university's premiere porticoed antebellum manor. We ran unhindered over the garden paths and through the laurel undergrowth.

Once, memorably, my family had dinner with the president, in the mansion, in the formal dining room, at the *cain't-see-the-end-of-it* formal table, with the secret foot bell beneath the head of the table, and we were allowed to crawl down underneath there to check it out, and press it, and thus summon the help, much to our surprise.

The days were sunny and the nights so soft and humid you could taste gentleness in the air.

Athens, Georgia 1955 Reconsidered

Sunny days and soft nights, but not everyone would sense gentleness.

Georgia Jim Crow laws enforcing segregation declared (among other similar prohibitions):

It shall be unlawful for a white person to marry anyone except a white person;

A restaurant shall serve either white people exclusively or colored people exclusively;

It shall be unlawful for colored people to frequent any park owned or maintained by the city for the benefit, use, and enjoyment of white persons;

No person controlling convicts shall confine white and colored convicts together, or work them chained together, or chain them together going to or from their work, or at any other time;

It shall be the duty of the board of education to make arrangements for the instruction of the children of the white and colored races in separate schools;

In order to ascertain whether an applicant is eligible for qualification as a voter ... the registrars shall orally propound to him the thirty questions on the standardized list.

April 29, 2005

Fifty years after my youthful nights in Georgia came the news.

ATLANTA (AP) - Gov. Sonny Perdue signed a set of bills Thursday that erased the last vestiges of Georgia's segregation-era Jim Crow laws

3. 1932 Detour

Expectations

On October 29, 1929, the US stock market fell like a wrecking ball split from its tether. The shock didn't faze my parents. For the moment they were sheltered by their love, and by the college. She with her job. He with his Master's studies.

Dad also had a job waiting for him in a Wisconsin lumber company's tree nursery, as soon as he graduated. Win and Don married in 1932 on the strength of the promise.

The job evaporated. Those were extraordinary times. WWI veterans were marching on the Capitol, wanting their service bonuses paid early. Hoovervilles—homeless encampments—were springing up around urban centers, and the police and army were ordered to attack the shanty-town in D.C.

With the Capitol City as backdrop, young American servicemen burned out their nation's own older battle-scarred veterans.

But my parents were both plucky and lucky. Unlike nearly a quarter of the workforce, Dad found work. With unemployment at its highest, when thousands of Southern Blacks were moving north in the Great Migration to find work and escape subjugation, Mom and Dad, both White, moved a thousand miles in the opposite direction, from Michigan to Florida, because Florida was where Dad found a spot.

Adding irony to irony in such a reverse migration, the position Dad had been promised in Wisconsin was re-offered as soon as he had accepted the state job in Florida, and before he and Mom started their move.

According to Mom, he was too principled to stay home and jilt the Florida Forest Service, so the two newlyweds moved to Lake City. Without those principles (which Mom later frequently offered as moral guidance) there would be no Southern branch of the Weddell clan.

A Year Later

The Depression caught up with them again. Florida started laying off state employees. When the state got to Dad, he and Mom went camping. When the state brought Dad back, but couldn't pay him, my parents, along with others, paid for necessities with scrip—local currency—which they got on the strength of their back wages.

And since they were leading a charmed life, Mom became pregnant in the fall of 1933.

From her telling, it is clear they were delighted. But the birth did not go well. When her labor was unproductive, the doctor only then found little Mary Winona lying in a breech position.

As Mom put it in a moment of rare candor, in terms graphically and ickily stuck in my brain, her *powers of expulsion failed*. The doctor had to reach in and hook his pinkie finger in Mary Win's tiny little jaw and try to pull her around and out at the same time, with both Mom and baby totally wrung out. Nine times out of ten the baby's neck was broken in such a desperate attempt. This was small-town panhandle Florida in 1934. There were no miracles of modern medicine. There was no modern medicine.

Mary Win was the one who made it.

Alabamy Bound

Mom and Dad were thankful and thrilled. Baby and mother had survived, the state was back to paying people, and furloughs were over. Life was fine with the Weddells.

Especially fine. Dad had a new job offer in Alabama. He was apparently both good at his job and ambitious. The new position was a big jump up from nurseryman (lowest White man in the Florida Forest Service chain of command) to assistant professor at the Alabama Polytechnic Institute, now Auburn University.

Auburn

Dead quiet.

That's not what you want at a party.

Mom was making quite a debut. The Agriculture Department had organized a welcome party, and someone thought Mom could play piano. She—normally vivacious and quick-witted, but not knowing anybody knew she played and thus unprepared—froze when asked to showcase her talent.

Then she found a major fault line and stomped on it. Sitting down at the keyboard, she offered up the first piece muscle-memory had to offer. A spirited version of *Marching Through Georgia*. With the first bars the fault opened and the party fell in.

A well-known tune, but well and universally detested by Southern Whites. A Union song from the end of the Civil War, joyfully, gleefully, celebrating a campaign of infamous war crimes.

Hurrah! Hurrah! we bring the jubilee!
Hurrah! Hurrah! the flag that makes you free!
o we sang the chorus from Atlanta to the sea

While we were marching through Georgia.

Seventy years later the scars from Sherman's march were tender as if it were yesterday, though the campaign ran through Georgia, not Alabama. Only a Yankee could have picked such a tune.

Amazingly, despite this wrong-footed start, Mom was forgiven, and some of the shocked, silence-stricken faculty went on to become her lifelong friends. They never mentioned it.

She told me.

The Southern Way of Life

It was Auburn where Mom fell in love with the South. Her living conditions were surely beyond her wildest expectations.

She liked the manners, the *yes ma'ams* and *no ma'ams*, the *pleases* and *thank yous*. The open-hearted hospitality and the slower pace. No mansion, like the one she would live near later on in Georgia, but the bungalow they were given rent-free was more than adequate for the three of them.

She loved learning the rules of genteel society and their Southern variations, and loved the pretty tea settings and salvers of her friends—inspiring her to start acquiring too.

There she grew fond of having servants. After Auburn, she was seldom without one. In Auburn, and around the country, times were still hard economically. But Dad's low pay in Auburn was supplemented by free help from the state, courtesy of the state justice system.

Black penitentiary trusties—inmates with special privilege—were provided to the new professor and his family as house and yard help. Mom's face as she told me this was warm, unusual for her, and full of affectionate memories.

I never worried about the trusties being convicts. They were reliable, nice, and well-behaved. I'm convinced they were, but there's a deeper backstory.

The Underside

The Southern way of life which some White people oohed and aahed about was for Whites only and was only made possible by our open and passionately defended racial subjugation of Black people, enforced by law and terror. Jim Crow and the Klan.

Mom and Dad never acknowledged this. When I asked Mom about racial tensions in her Michigan hometowns, she said *We didn't have any colored people.* I think the statement implied to her *How could I be prejudiced if there weren't any coloreds?*

Mom's Alabama trusties? Part of the underbelly. The Southern penal system extended and reinforced the Jim Crow laws—its effects on Black people and their communities analogous to the way today's War on Drugs works.

Under Southern justice, Blacks were charged, prosecuted, and convicted more often than Whites for similar offenses. They served longer sentences and did so in harsher institutions.

Becoming a trusty was a way to ease those longer sentences and the harder time which Blacks served, if not the disproportional way they wound up in prison. To the wardens and the state, having trusties meant lowering prison costs, and opening up more routes for smuggling, bribery, and coercion.

Being an outside-the-walls house servant was the best trusty spot available. Light duty, especially compared to prison farm labor or chain-gang work, and the ability to move about outside the walls. In contrast, inside-the-walls trusty jobs could be dangerous and brutal. *The Shooter*, who killed other prisoners trying to escape, was the highest of those.

19

It would be rare for a prisoner to jeopardize his privileged house or yard-servant trusty position. For inmates in those spots the work made the best of a bad situation. However, the system as a whole was a cesspool of favoritism, cruelty, sleaze, and venality.

And yet it survived until 1974, when it was found to violate prisoners' rights under the First, Sixth, Eighth, and Fourteenth Amendments to the Constitution. That's a lot of amendments.

An old-time governor of Mississippi, James K. Vardaman, said his prison was run *like an efficient slave plantation.*

When he said it, in the early 1900s, he meant it as praise.

Mary Win

About the time Mary Win was learning to walk, my parents noticed she seemed weak and ran out of breath quickly. Having ducked tragedy in Lake City they thought they were out of the fight. But they weren't; they were only started.

As Mary Win's physical difficulties became more obvious—turning blue before the other kids did in the cold or the water, tiring much sooner than the other kids—and her mental development started lagging behind, my folks became more and more concerned, and started searching for answers.

The first explanation they heard from a doctor stuck with Mom. She took it as her fault. What she heard was something like this *when your powers of expulsion failed, Mary Win's oxygen was cut off and her brain damaged.* How the doctor worded his explanation to Mom isn't known, but *failed* was the word she used.

She took the weight of the culture's expectations on her shoulders. By not producing a healthy child she would feel she let her husband down, flopping both as a good wife and as a good mother.

I don't always take Mom's side, but she was unfair to herself. Mary Win's symptoms, including those diagnosed later, are also, and I think better, explained by Down Syndrome.

But, I also think Mom would have taken Down Syndrome on her shoulders too. In addition to the heft of societal expectations, Mom carried her family's strong flavor of depression. Her self-blame for Mary Win's differentness was a hint of something coming down the road.

I never got the sense Dad was remorseful about Mom and Mary Win. Whatever else happened in our family, when he was with us there was always a feeling he loved us all. There was not a sign he held Mary Win's conditions against Mom, or blamed her for Mary Win's limitations. Or that he didn't love Mary Win as much as he loved the rest of us.

That first doctor didn't explain Mary Win's physical symptoms, just her mental ones. A woman less susceptible to guilt and less in awe of doctors might have heard those pronouncements and wondered if maybe something else than her own *failure* might be at work there. But that wasn't my mom.

Travelin' Man (and Daughter)

Dad was not satisfied with the Auburn doctor's explanation, and he and Mom decided to check out Atlanta's MDs. Dad, unusually so for a man of his generation, was devoted to his daughter and it showed in this effort.

In Mom's telling of the story, she gives him the credit for taking the lead in seeking out specialists and arranging the trips. (Eerie for me to hear, because I knew the roles had been reversed before he died, and Mom had been the one working with doctors to find something to stop the high blood pressure from killing him.)

But in their visit to Atlanta, it was more of the same. Brain damage due to the breech presentation and long delivery. Nothing about the shortness of breath and general weakness. However, the doctors there did suggest they go, if they could, to Johns Hopkins.

Mom and Dad must have been daunted. They were from rural Michigan. They had moved to rural Florida and next to a small college town in Alabama. They didn't have money or connections, and Johns Hopkins in Baltimore was the nation's first teaching hospital and the most prestigious medical institution in the country.

It must have been a tough decision. They could get good news, bad news, or the same muddle, and it would be an arduous trip.

It would also eat up most of their meager finances. Mom's story always implied Mary Win and Dad made the trip without her. Finances would have been the reason. Her anxiety while they were gone would have been extreme. Mom never said whether Dad and Mary Win made the eight-hundred-mile trip by train or car, but either was a long trip in the 1930s. Dad loved to travel. No one could know how Mary Win would take to it.

Answers

Old and new. The Johns Hopkins team agreed with brain-damage-from-breech-birth explaining slow mental development. However, they found a faulty heart valve no one else had suspected to account for the physical weakness.

There was a big *but* though. Heart valve repair wasn't possible yet in the states. There was *one* experimental surgery in the early 1920s. Afterward the procedure was considered unjustified. Doctors wouldn't resume heart valve surgery until the late 1940s, after WWII. The family had more information, but no more options.

So Dad and Mary Win came back to Mom in Auburn, with nothing obviously changed. There was, nonetheless, a subterranean shift occurring. Not that they hadn't been careful with her before, but now they knew she had a weak heart, life would be different.

That new understanding would alter the way they dealt with Mary Win, shift their lives, and eventually mark mine.

Moves

1939. Hitler took over Poland. Sherman marched through Georgia yet again in the film version of *Gone with the Wind*. Dad took over the Georgia Division of Forestry.

It seemed like such a great opportunity my folks may not have done their homework. In the previous eight Depression-filled years, 117 state departments had been winnowed to seventeen. Eight district forestry offices had been cut to four. And state foresters were not lasting long in office.

Dad continued the trend.

He stayed barely long enough to catch the eyes of University of Georgia administrators searching for a new Dean of Forestry. Within months the Weddells had pulled up stakes and moved to a rental home in Athens—apparently leaving behind no hard feelings, since part of Dad's new responsibilities would be to work closely with his former (but brief) employer, the state Division of Forestry.

The family seemed to find what they wanted in Athens and at the University. Mom had been embraced by the Faculty Wives' Club, gotten her overall bearings, and she and Dad decided it would be OK if she went back to work.

Mary Win was five and capable of being baby-sat. Black help—while not complimentary courtesy of a state pen—was inexpensive and available for housework and minding children. Mom's new friends would help her find someone and advise her about wages and local customs.

23

Her salary would cover the help easily and leave more than enough to contribute to the family budget. Her credentials and Dad's connections found her a position almost immediately in the agricultural college, and the family was off. Making a new life again.

Five years later—eleven years following Mary Wins arrival—Caroline Elizabeth was born. Two and a half years later I completed the family. Mom and Dad left the rental house behind, built a new house to their design, acquired a succession of dogs and cats, and thought they had settled down for the long haul. They had, but the haul wasn't going to be as long as they thought.

4. The Shade of Thirteen Oaks

A Child's Life

Athens' heat and humidity never bothered me. But since I'd never lived anywhere else, I didn't know it could be different.

We had no air conditioning in the house, but we had the shelter of a baker's dozen leafy oak trees and a fan to circulate the air. I saw snow only a time or two. Everything shut down and the grown-ups ran their cars into each other's trying to get home. Like bumper cars at the fair, only without any apparent fun. Once the school board closed the schools for cold. There wasn't any snow, just cold.

Much of the year we'd play outside past dark. By porchlights, street-lights, and no lights we'd play Tag, Blind Man's Bluff, Mother, May I? Ain't No Bugger Man Out Tonight, Red Light-Green Light, and any game we could make up. (Sling the Statues, for instance. One kid slung each of the other kids around and let go. The kid who landed resembling whatever the Slinger claimed to have been thinking of became the new Slinger.)

The closest thing to a moral dilemma we faced was whether to go barefoot so we could enjoy the feel of the damp grass on our feet or whether to put on shoes to avoid the disgusting feeling when you stepped on something moist and squishy and sticky like a slug—or worse.

Athens was the kind of place, and we lived on the kind of street, where you could, and we did, lie down in the street gutter and let warm summer rainwater wash right over us. Caroline and I once strung a rope across the street and played tennis with two warped hand-me-down cat-gut tennis rackets.

Having traffic light and slow enough to allow a rope across a street is rare now, but years ago our surprise was finding enough rope to go completely across. Cloverhurst, the street we lived on, was extraordinarily wide for a residential street. Once it was the private drive for a Victorian mansion, a misbegotten two-story pile of poorly sorted windows, gables, turrets, tower, and an unfortunate covered porch guaranteeing a gloomy interior.

Instead of mansions, my friends lived in commonplace single-family houses like ours. When Dad died we took in roomers to make ends meet, but none of my friends had paying guests. Athens, as I knew it, was Dick and Jane turf, and we had no cognitive dissonance with our grammar-school reading books.

The one-family houses, the picket fences, the White kids running on tree-shaded sidewalks with their dogs were real as my skin. It wasn't until an urban refugee (later my wife) explained it to me that I understood how foreign my world was to her.

She had the same reading book, but its small-town focus made no sense to her growing up in a ninth-floor New York City apartment.

Run Spot, run! The Mercer Street gang is after our lunch money.

Somehow those words never made it into our primers.

Plantation Woods

Trees and brush filled the left-behind parcel. Almost. A neglected scuppernong arbor—barely domesticated wild grapes supported uneasily on rusty steel trellis-work—still stood. A similarly neglected, yet stately and bearing, pecan tree was not surrendering to time or creeping undergrowth.

26

And looming through the vegetation at the back corner, the wounded Civil War-era mansion, to which the parcel once belonged.

Two-story-tall Doric columns lined the veranda, while a granite block waited patiently at the front curb for long-missing carriages: a century back in time this was one of Athens' jewels, the family seat of the Carltons. In 1943, when Mom and Dad were exploring the manse's woodlot, the historic structure was barely getting by serving as an unkempt fraternity house.

Two Carltons still lived nearby. The oldest surviving sister lived in an incongruous small brick house adjacent to the big house. The younger sister, Miss Annie, lived close to hand, surrounded by magnolia trees on another piece of the old estate. She was the one who had agreed to let my folks ramble through her old play grounds and perhaps buy them. It worked out well for everyone.

****

I believe those trees were important. Dad needed them to surround his soul. Forestry was more than a job for him. Woods and wood (and family) were his loves. And Mom needed no coaxing. They had spent their courtship not bowling, but camping.

A waterfall in the woods was where he proposed. In Athens Dad got trees and wood, not asphalt and brick. Mom got Dad at peace, trees, and her dream house.

And we, the kids, got a magical place in which to grow up.

****

You forgot something. Don't leave out the slave quarters behind the bighouse, Caroline reminds me.

What slave house?

Find those baby pictures I sent you. The ones with you in the crib in the backyard. The slave house is partly hidden by the hedge behind you.

Oh, I remember. When we were taking the shortcut home from high school and cutting across behind the big-house, it was sitting there like nobody had remembered to knock it down.

And don't forget the stone-walled well, either. We had to walk right by it. It scared us, like it would suck us into the well if we got any closer.

Open House

Surrounded by oaks, dogwoods, redbuds, and photinia, our parent-designed story-and-a-half Cape Codder had a large attic bedroom with three dormer windows for Caroline and me to share. On the same level, two more attics and a bathroom also clustered around the upstairs hall. We got there by climbing an oak-trimmed, banistered staircase—going down, it doubled as a sliding board. *Thump, thump, thump.*

Downstairs, the stairway turned neatly to land beside the front door and point you toward the living room. There Mom's decorating taste ran into the tendency of boys to break easily broken treasures.

More than once I did that, playing solo indoor catch by bouncing a tennis ball off the upper risers of the stairs and trying to field the rebound while standing on the landing. Behind me on the wall was a knickknack shelf. Some of the breakage could be glued back together with Duco cement. Some couldn't.

Caroline and I summered on the back porch which opened off the living room through French doors. It was almost like camping. We could sleep without a fan, watch the fireflies, and catch the shadows creeping across the lawn. One morning Caroline said *Look at the fireplace. No not the front. Around on the side, at the middle rock.*

I only see a flat rock.

28

Look above the flat rock.

Oh, I got it. The one like a face. You think it's painted?

Yeah, what do you think?

Yeah, me too.

The rock was mainly rock, but some areas were emphasized with colors almost matching the rest of the stones but more intense. A dark-bearded man's face in profile appeared. He was peering out at the backyard stern and alert. I thought he looked like a younger Dad with a beard and sideburns. Caroline thought it was Abe Lincoln.

Then we went on a search. There was one more, a suggestion, like maybe the mystery painter saw a radish-shaped nose barely projecting from the rock and whispered the vision with a bare hint of help from paints. This stoneface was goofy, with his vegetable nose, a round-shaped rock head, and not much hair. Charlie Brown grown old. Could a rock be bald? And have pale blue, almost gray eyes?

The Attic Mystery

The smallest attic exerted a dangerous pull. Caroline and I knew it had no windows and knew its rock-wool insulation was leaking from the rafters. We presumed the monsters. But we went in anyway, our skin drawing tight in anticipation of both a scare and an itch from the rock-wool.

Our presumed dangerous-creations-with-ill-intentions lurked in the shadowed recesses, and to keep them there we had to turn on the light. Finding the switch would involve feeling around by the door where we'd inevitably touch the exposed cloth-covered wiring before we found what we were searching for. If we succeeded in finding the switch without frying ourselves, we would turn on only one badly placed, low-wattage, dust-covered bulb.

But once our eyes adjusted, we seemed safer. We knew monsters were afraid of even this small shy light, and what threatening shapes we could see turned into familiar old clothes in and out of bags, my old crib (*It was my crib. You stole it from me,* Caroline maintains), a bassinet, Dad's movie projector and screen, abandoned luggage, and a little room with a door.

It was the little room within the attic that was mysterious, not the monsters. We knew about monsters from reading. But what was a three-foot square room doing there? It was merely bare-studded onto the nearest corner, off-handedly out of place. But inside it had finished interior walls, a light and a light switch (with a cover-plate and buried wiring), and strangely, a toilet.

I tried the toilet, more than once, and it worked fine. But what was the point? There was a perfectly nice bathroom entered from the hall, sharing a common wall with this little hideaway afterthought.

Why did this toilet exist? For the monsters? Another puzzle I couldn't solve was the sun-colored box of Arm & Hammer baking soda open on the toilet tank.

Why was it there? Caroline didn't know, so I asked Mom. A last resort. Her answer: *It's Beulah Mae's toilet.*

No help there. Why did Beulah Mae get a special toilet? I gathered somehow Mom also meant *You're not to use it.* Well, too late for that. And she said the soda box helped with the smell.

What smell? I wondered. The attic simply smelled dusty to me, and this was the first I'd heard of baking soda having anything to do with smells. I thought it was for cooking.

So that's how Mom and I left it. I figured I wasn't going to get anything understandable out of her, so I wouldn't try again, but I also figured I could therefore pretend I didn't get Mom's hint about not using *Beulah Mae's* toilet. What about when Caroline was tying up the bathroom and I needed to go? It didn't seem right to let a perfectly good toilet go to waste.

30

Besides, how come Beulah Mae got her own bathroom while Caroline and I had to share?

Ronnie

In the spring of 1955, as I pedaled home from the drugstore and an adventure in Southern etiquette, I wasn't thinking far into the future, mainly daydreaming about lying down on the living room sofa with a bag of potato chips and a Coke and reading *Lone Ranger* cover to cover, including all the ads.

Had I uncharacteristically thought further ahead, I would never have guessed my life would change so drastically, for good and bad, in such a short time.

The good came first.

In the fall of the year, Dad hired a new faculty member at the forestry school. I heard about it over the dinner table, but it didn't concern me so I didn't pay much attention, missing the mention of a kid around my age.

They lived on the other side of town. Normal Town we called it, because in the dim past that's where the Normal School had been. Of course I didn't have a clue what *Normal School* meant, but in time someone explained about a school out there, once separate from the university, to teach girls to become teachers. In '55 it was home to the US Naval Supply Corps school.

For a kid it was a confusing name for a part of town. What did having a Normal Town make those of us who lived elsewhere?

Anyway, Ronnie—the new faculty member's son—and I finally met at the Y, where I spent as much time as I could. Norman Rockwell painted this kid more than once. He had red hair and freckles, a slingshot in his back pocket, a grin on his face, and you knew he would be absolutely deaf to his mother's call.

We fought to a draw on the Y wrestling mats and were best friends after, without ever thinking about it or saying anything about it. Not only was Ronnie's dad a forester like mine, but Ronnie had a younger sister who was a little bit like Mary Win. Not a lot, but a little. If Mom hadn't mentioned it I'm not sure I would have known, but I don't think she would be wrong about something like that.

Ronnie's redbrick house sat on a steeply sloping lot with a kudzu-filled ravine at the bottom, and though it appeared to be a one-story house from the front, the basement sat like another main floor facing backwards. It had windows and doors exactly like the upstairs, and while now I know to call it a daylight basement, it was the first such setup I'd ever seen.

I'd come in the front door; we'd go downstairs like we were going to play inside, and instead head right for the ravine. A lot simpler than asking permission or telling somebody where we were going.

A little-known fact: there's no time/space continuum issue with having two Tarzans at the same time in the same place. No fancy time machines or teleporters or molecular defibrillators, or anything required. You can do it because you're both there in the ravine in shorts without any shirts on, and there's this huge river with crocodiles and snakes and cataracts, cleverly disguised as a piddly-ass creek, and there're the kudzu vines. So barely ahead of the thundering elephant stampede, you grab a vine and swing across the river. Safe on the other side.

Of course, you could wind up with one of you left behind in mortal danger because his vine didn't swing—always a danger with kudzu vines. In which case you have to swing back to rescue him, which might involve, just might, swinging right into him, and knocking him down, and both of you collapsing in hysterical laughter.

And about that time you might hear Jo, Ronnie's mom, calling for you. But more likely you wouldn't hear her.

Ronnie never did, so I didn't either.

Jo

There was something different about Jo. She had a disappearing temper. She got loudly mad. And *boom!* she got over it. I'd never seen anything like it. Loud-voice mad and over it. Quickly. It seemed so simple.

In my house, from Mom you got disapproval and guilt-pushing, unanswerable questions like *Why'd you leave the water running?* How do you answer that? *Because I'm stupid? Because I'm forgetful? Because I'm a kid?* and her displeasure seemed to last forever. She was often cross, but rarely direct. And if what you'd done was genuinely bad she might tell Dad when he got home.

But temper wasn't the only trait different with Jo. There seemed to be an understanding between her and Ronnie. He would ignore her calls and her instructions and go do whatever he wanted, but at some point we'd go back to the house and get yelled at, and that would be that. We'd eat our sandwiches, finish, and run outside for more adventures.

Playing at Ronnie's house was a freeing experience.

One More Thing about Jo

Jo was petite, but her spirit made her seem bigger. She had black hair, dark eyes, freckles like Ronnie's but fewer of them, a trim figure, and a huge temper. But not an unreasonable one. I loved the *easy come, easy go* nature of it. I hoped it would never be directed at me. I would wilt. Disappear on the spot.

She understood Ronnie, and for myself, her understanding him meant she would understand me. Ronnie and I were like long-lost twin brothers when I was at their house. I lost my worries about pleasing people and making mistakes. Ronnie and Jo made it possible.

But there were parts of Jo I figured out only later, much later. First, she was young compared to my mom and my other friends' moms. Should have understood the age difference sooner. The second part was genuinely harder. I didn't have the word much less the concept as a kid, which is good. But it was an interesting moment when I did grasp it. Oh, *that's* what *that* was about! She was young, good-looking, vivacious and ... *sexy*.

Sidebar for Mary Win

Ronnie lived with his sister Sandy differently than we did with Mary Win. We were careful with Mary Win. He treated Sandy like a pest.

They'd yell at each other and get mad, a bit shy of hair-pulling is what it seemed (which Ronnie would win if it happened, because he had a buzz cut and Sandy had girl hair). When they ran out of words they'd storm off in different directions.

I didn't know what Sandy would do next because of course I stormed off with Ronnie, but as soon as we were away from her he was done being mad. It seemed more like what most people thought was a normal big brother/little sister relationship. A lot of teasing, and *no, you can't come* on his part and trying to tag along on her part, and fighting, but nothing weird, though I was told Sandy was different.

In those younger years I'd not understood something important about them, Ronnie and Sandy, something I missed with Mary Win.

They fulfilled the other side of the big brother/little sister stereotype. The part where there is an uncomplicated love underneath the squabbling and teasing, and where they watch out for each other. My family did the watching-after piece well.

But except for Dad, who seemed to get it right, the love was anything but simple.

The Family Contract

In our family Caroline tried to protect me; I tried to look after her; Mary Win tried to mommy both of us, and Caroline and I together tried to care for Mary Win when we grew into it. Now I can see what I took as unwelcome mothering from Mary Win was her way of caring for her little brother.

Before I grew into a more caring soul I thought the family understanding with Mary Win was too one-sided. Because Mary Win was special and fragile, we tended to walk on eggshells around her. When Mom thought I was old enough to understand, she explained it to me, but mainly it was a given. *Mary Win gets her way. Try not to cross her. She's got a bad heart and her mind won't grow like yours. It's a miracle she's alive. Don't mess it up.*

That's what I heard. Mom handled it opaquely, minced a lot of words, and would never have put it so baldly, but I got it. I had for years.

Unmentioned about Mary Win was the occasional mean temper.

Temper, Temper

My oldest sister was an avid fan of Lawrence Welk's TV variety show. It featured big-band dance music, vocalists, and dancers, and created the light, family-friendly "Champagne Music" genre.

Myself, I liked westerns (a torch I carried from a long romance with all things cowboy) and mysteries. However, I would frequently deign to watch Welk with her. The demographic this show hit and held nicely for years was forties-plus. Not cool for boys my age, which at the time of this story — 1959 — was twelve.

Rawhide, a now-classic western series, was normally on against *The Lawrence Welk Show*, so I rarely saw it. But one evening when I was

35

spinning the dial I found *Rawhide* on in a special slot, the beginning of a two-part special. (TVs in the 50s had a numbered knob for changing channels. The moveable outer ring of the knob was the fine tuner. We picked our signal out of the air.)

I was hooked. *Rawhide* had a grittiness totally opposed to the wholesome likes of the Roy Rogers/Dale Evans western husband and wife routine which our family once had watched together.

Sitting in front of the Roy Rogers show we didn't fret about 1900s cowboys and cowgirls dressing in square-dance high-fashion while packing six-shooters. Or worry about turn-of-the-century characters merrily encountering and using cars, electric lights, and landline phones. Or fuss about a comic-relief Jeep with a mind of its own.

Perhaps the anachronisms, stock characters, and poor acting were part of its charm. You knew who was who and how it would turn out. Goodness and virtue would prevail. Since Dad died, the world I saw wasn't always like that.

****

I had to see *Rawhide's* Part Two. Something had resonated. But the show was back on in its normal slot against Lawrence Welk.

I made my plan. I would get to the TV first and *problem solved*.

Mary Win would miss Lawrence Welk, but she could catch him the next week. I could catch Part Two the night it aired or never.

That first and only part of the plan went off without a hitch.

I was on the floor in front of the TV before Mary Win arrived, and had the TV turned on and tuned in before my show began. I thought the problem was licked. I was there first. The *Rawhide* theme song rolled.

Move 'em out, head 'em up,

Head 'em up, move 'em on.

Move 'em out, head 'em up: Rawhiiide!

****

Predictably—to anyone other than me—my plan fell apart immediately.

Mary Win came in and switched the channel. I turned it back. She switched it again. I turned it back. We both started yelling. No one in our house ever yelled. We ran for Mom.

In the dining room we faced off again. Out of control I feverishly quaked *You can see Lawrence Welk next week! I can only see my show tonight!* She screamed at me *NO! I watch Lawrence Welk!* grabbing a ballpoint pen and jamming it at my head. I dodged reflexively.

By which time, I was in tears and my show had started without me. Mary Win stomped off to watch Welk, and Mom showed up to do what she could to patch our spat.

There wasn't much she could do. She wasn't going to fight with Mary Win and I wasn't going to acknowledge how much I hated Mary Win always getting her way and how she was so special—it would have seemed too mean-spirited and ungrateful. But I was going to miss the show.

Inconsolable, I didn't want to admit my fright, nor how ashamed I was of my tears. I never thought Mary Win would try to hurt me.

Mom took me in her arms and sat me in her lap in her rocker, the thinly padded pink one she had cuddled me in when I was small and upset. She soothed me and rocked me. I was entirely too big to be rocked, but it helped some. At the same time it made me feel weak and babyish.

We never mentioned it again.

5. Change

Beginning

I had no inkling Dad was going to die.

I knew Mom worried about his high blood pressure, but I had only a vague idea of what it was. She worried about so much—my skinniness, were the windows clean, Caroline's friend problems, Mary Win's health, was Grandmother's braided-rag rug out of place in the living room, should she let me play tackle football—I didn't understand the worry about Dad was something worth worrying about.

Dad might not have recognized it either. While I always wanted him to play with me more, to throw a ball around, or roughhouse (which he never did), he may have thought he had all the time in the world to play with the children.

Or maybe he couldn't do it because of his high blood pressure. But when he was around he was loving, warm, and playful, quite different from Mom. He'd tote us around in a pool or a lake, on his shoulders or in a tube, and he introduced us to the joys of water play—fishing, rowing, swimming, and hanging out in the water or on the shore. Sometimes on Saturday morning he'd catch us still in our PJs and rub his rough stubble against our soft kid faces. We'd squeal and grimace, but we loved the attention.

He made us toys, too. He was handy with old boards, hammers, and saws. He'd make us little boats to float down the creek where we had family picnics right in town, and he made us a fine big church to go with the Lionel train set he gave us one Christmas.

When he was with us it didn't seem there was enough of him to go around.

Middle

Dad became different in 1955.

At first, it was life as usual. I was in third grade by '55, and playing tackle football at the Y. Every couple of weeks we would play a night game and parents would come. Mom came, but he never did.

By the time basketball season arrived, Dad's non-appearance at my little events was like an itch I couldn't scratch. I craved more Dad. Finally, when we were scheduled to play a visiting team from nearby Commerce, Dad promised to come to the game.

Dad had always been too busy. Mom stood up for him. *He is the dean, you know, and a Kiwanis lieutenant governor and both of those mean he has to go to a lot of evening meetings.*

I didn't care. The only thing I comprehended about meetings was since we didn't see him much except on weekends, I didn't like meetings.

****

At Y basketball games parents sat on the unused indoor running track over the basketball court. For the Commerce game Dad was going to be up there. There was no other place he could be, because there was maybe three feet between the court boundaries and the brick walls of the 1919 building.

(That old running track presented its own challenges for players. It arced over part of the court. Any shot from any corner needed a flat trajectory, otherwise it would be deflected by the underside of the track. Knowing that fact of Athens Y basketball gave us a distinct homecourt advantage.)

When the game was about to start I looked up from the mat room where the players were gathered right next to the court and I didn't see Dad. Not caring about being conspicuous, I ran across the court to the far side so I could see the other side of the running track. *Nope, not there either.* I saw Mom though, but her being there didn't count. I wanted Dad. Maybe I didn't spot him. Those were not tears welling in my eyes.

After the game he didn't appear when Mom did. Those were still not tears welling up. *Where was Dad?* I demanded. *He had to leave for a meeting,* she admitted. *He did come. He got here a little after the start, and stayed most of the time. He said to say he was sorry he couldn't see it all.*

I was deflated. Mom rattled on while I thought, *It isn't the same if he was there and I didn't know it.*

****

He might not have been there at all. Mom might have covered for him. She would have done that, if he had blown the game off.

He never asked me anything about the game, and I never spoke to him about it either. Who knows, if I had spoken, we might have become closer. But it would be a long time before I would talk about my little wounds, or my big ones.

****

The changes started when our mild winter ended.

Spring comes early in Georgia, and one warmish day Dad came home accompanied by a truck. He had somehow wrangled a refrigerator shipping box, sensing its possibilities.

I couldn't wait for Ronnie to come over and see what we had to play with. When he got there we got Dad's hammers and beat two of the planks loose, followed by pounding and pulling the nails out and

41

straightening them for future use. That's what we always did with nails back then.

What nail removal left us with was two planks seemingly like the rest, but planks we who knew the secret could remove and crate an opening for slipping into the fort. Completing our security measures from inside the clubhouse we slipped the nail-less planks back into place and nobody could find us, or how to get into the crate. It looked like merely an old crate behind the garage.

Ronnie and I knew better. It was actually an army bunker.

If worse came to worst and the Japanese or the Germans threatened to overrun our position, we could retreat out of the fort, clamber from its roof to the top of the neighbor's toolshed, then hoist ourselves up to the eave of our garage and belly crawl the rest of the way up to the ridge of the garage where we controlled the high ground. From there we were invincible.

We could either mow the phantom enemy down with the wooden machine gun I fashioned myself, or we could pretend-parachute onto them by jumping off the roof. Our enemies never learned. They always attacked right over the huge decomposing leaf pile a leap into space away from the edge of the roof.

Occasionally one of us would die. Sometimes both of us. We'd mainly die silently, but very, very realistically. This was a skill much admired by third grade boys. So you had to die fairly frequently to stay in practice.

****

We played army, not navy, not Tarzan, and not cowboys. Ronnie must have led the switch since cowboy mania was still with me, but it was a good change of rhythm. We played army, but we wanted to be sailors.

I asked my Dad about the war once, and he told me the safest place to be in a war was on a ship, and I believed him. Ronnie's dad, Ron, Sr., had been on a ship in the war. In my mind he was the captain of a destroyer. He had a picture of the ship in his and Jo's bedroom. It was cool, a black-and-white photo of the ship under steam, only the ship, the sea, the sky, and a sense of purpose. Despite the parental leanings, it was hard to play navy in a dry backyard.

****

More surprise. There hadn't been a kid-and-Dad trip in our family since Mary Win and Dad went to Johns Hopkins. But later in the spring of '56, Dad took Caroline on a trip to Washington, D.C.

The rest of us saw them off at the train depot on the edge of town. Air travel hadn't reached the middle-class (or Athens) yet, and since we had no expectations of flying, trains were exciting. The family loved the depot.

At Dad's suggestion we'd drive down of a Saturday evening to watch the trains come in. Dad's dad had been a railroad man in the late 1800s on what in due course became the Soo Line Railroad. I think that's where Dad picked up his familiarity and ease with trains and depots, although, if so, he picked it up young. Dad was only fifteen when his dad died.

When we got to the depot, Dad would park the Oldsmobile in the gravel lot beside the concrete apron and Caroline and I would pop out and run to play on the big wooden freight wagons, our heads barely above their decks.

Their steel wheels were chained so we couldn't push them far, but there was enough slack to allow one of us to ride about six feet while the other one pushed. At six feet the end of the slack would jerk the wagon to a kid-bouncing stop, and we'd reverse roles.

When we became bored with wagon-play and with checking-out the waiting room — already antique in 1956 — we'd skip down the tracks toward Atlanta and put a penny on the rails for the streamliner to flatten.

43

You could feel the train coming before you could see it. The elevated pulse vibrated our little bodies, and those bodies translated the pounding as *Danger!* We'd think to each other, as happened occasionally, *Are Mom and Dad sure this is safe?*

The train that *thummed* through our little bodies was our favorite, Seaboard Railroad's Silver Comet, passing through Athens on its run from New York to Birmingham and back. Caroline and Dad would make the run to Washington in about twelve hours, mostly sleeping, and would have two whole days in Washington sightseeing and staying with a friend of our folks.

It was years before I set foot on a train, but I wasn't jealous Caroline was going to spend two nights in a Pullman sleeper and eat in the dining car each way.

I was jealous of her time with Dad.

****

The friend was Mena, you remember her? Caroline prods. *Mena visited Athens once. In Washington she and Dad spent a lot of time whispering in the kitchen when they thought I couldn't hear, and when they thought I was asleep. Do you think they were having an affair?*

No. No hesitation on my part.

Caroline takes the irreligious suspicion back. *I don't now, but I wondered about it when I grew up. Now I think Dad was worried about his health and needed somebody to talk to.*

****

Dad didn't stop there with his new-found kid-centric behavior—the clubhouse for me and the trip for Caroline. He brought Mary Win a new record player from D.C.

The record player was an important part of her daily life, and it was worn out. Miles and miles of circular travel, making pop music, musicals, and Christian standards spring out of black vinyl. The music alternated with teaching her imaginatively created school class and swaying gently in the swing Dad suspended from a big oak out back. She didn't mind if Caroline and I used the swing, but we knew it was hers.

That school class was something no one pried into. All we saw was the outside. Mary Win sitting in the swing or on the front porch talking softly to unseen kids, and occasionally marking something down in a teacher's gradebook with her cartridge ink pen.

Mom bought the grade books downtown, and Mary Win would fill them with students' names, their attendance, and their grades. I never listened to her classes, but now I'd like to know more. Once or twice I peeked at the books and could recognize a name or two of her friends from school and church.

A few weeks after Caroline, Dad, the record player, and a model airplane with wheels which spun the propellers got back from D. C., there was another surprise. Dad and Ron Senior took me and Ronnie to forestry field camp.

It was heaven. They let us run free at Hard Labor Creek, the state park where the camp was held, and we watched the college boys compete in pole-climbing, birling, axe-throwing, log-rolling with peaveys, cross-cut sawing, and canoe jousting. We used the taller-than-we-were peaveys ourselves and managed a quite respectable showing, we thought, rolling the knotty, unpeeled log up and down the field. And we came home with a trophy, at least it was to us. One of the jousting poles (two-by-twos with rubber toilet plunger ends) broke during battle, and we were awarded the stub.

There was more. Another boys'-day-out trip with our dads down to Warm Springs—the place that FDR went to soothe his pain. Warm Springs was south of us and toward Alabama, where again they let us roam on our own while they talked to the landowner about his woodlands.

Our dads' trust in us this time was misplaced. Ronnie and I found an (optimistically assumed to be) abandoned farmhouse and proceeded to blissfully destroy all the window panes we could with a barrage of acorns and chestnuts.

Sometimes I admit, *What abandoned house is nicely painted and still has its glass?*

End

With only three days left in the '55-'56 school year, and summer vacation on the near horizon, I was playing with my neighborhood friend Bubbie in yet another kudzu jungle, while Dad was in the hospital with his high blood pressure.

This jungle was like the one behind Ronnie's house, only bigger. The creek was bigger too, and upstream was an abandoned swimming pool. Downstream was a cave in the creek bank. We were in the cave. About two or three boys big, it was solid clay.

Bubbie and I were squishing the clay between our fingers and making clayballs, when the Olds blared its horn. It was Mom. I ran up the hill through the brush and the kudzu and jumped into the massive beast. We were going to the hospital to see Dad.

He'd been in St. Mary's before and visiting him was fun. I was born there and I got to see nuns. While they were scary, it was daring, like walking slowly by the graveyard at night. The old brick building was creaky and easy to get lost in, so I wanted to go. When I hopped in the car, Mom took one peek at my clay-streaked face, arms, legs, pants, and shirt, and said *No, you're too dirty. Walk home and clean up. You can go tomorrow.*

There was no tomorrow for Dad.

When I woke up the next morning, a preacher I hardly knew was in my room telling me to wake up and get dressed.

Jimmy, you're the man of the family now and you have to take care of your mom. Your dad died last night.

He stood awkwardly by the foot of the bed for a moment before sidling away gawkily. Sort of soured me on preachers.

I cried some, not nearly enough. I didn't know what it meant. I didn't know how to feel. Even what I was supposed to feel. But there was nothing there. I was empty and numb inside. I went downstairs and the grown-ups filled the living room. Nobody paid me much attention.

I didn't know where Caroline was, or Mary Win, or Mom, or what I was supposed to do, or how I was supposed to act. But another one of the hardly known grown-ups came over and said I was going to Ronnie's. That put a smile on my face. And my world started to right itself.

But when she said *Mary Win is coming too* the smile fell off. I sat around till Jo, Ronnie, and Sandy drove up, and Mary Win and I piled into their bulbously squat, gray-gone-to-worse Plymouth sedan. We drove in silence over to the familiar redbrick house on Edwards Circle. Jo and the girls went inside, and Ronnie and I stayed out and played as if nothing was different. It was the first time I could breathe all day.

I was comfortable and at home and didn't have to think about anything. We went to the ravine and swung on the vines, and the elephants did a special stampede for us, and we (Ronnie, me, and the elephants) had a mindlessly good time.

Then we went out front to see if orange-headed Van was at his house, because he was fun too. On the way I heard Jo calling, but Ronnie, as usual, didn't. Van wasn't home so we headed back to Ronnie's — pausing first to throw stones at the stop sign. Mary Win was waiting for me in front of the house. She was mad. Stomping her little foot and screeching incoherently. Ronnie couldn't understand a word she was saying, but I could. She was telling me off for not coming when Jo called. My safe little alternate life at Ronnie's house ended too.

****

The day continued to be a loser when Mary Win and I returned home in the evening.

I had managed to forget my bewilderment when Ronnie was by my side (and Mary Win wasn't), but being home brought it back. I was being brave, but it was costing me—inside I was reduced to confused, sad mush.

Mom convened a discussion almost as soon as we got in the door. We didn't sit down. *Do you want to go the funeral?* No preamble, no hugs, no going to the kitchen table, no Cokes to drink. Bang. *Do you want to go to the funeral?*

I was still smarting from being separated from Mom and Caroline all day. It seemed like Mom didn't want me around, didn't want to see me, didn't want to think how I might not be OK.

Her misery and uncertain functioning the days before the funeral and the weeks following left me with the belief she spent her whole first day in shock and grief, thinking only about herself.

****

No, you're wrong, Caroline asserts. *Mom spent the day tending to details, calling to let people know, working on the obituary and death notice, greeting people who came by, accepting their casseroles and condolences. There's a lot to do when somebody dies.*

Maybe a little too hot, I tossed back at Caroline, *What's more important*

48

than taking care of her children? I was only eight, you were only eleven, Mary Win—who knows how old she was in her head, but she needed something too.

****

I was not able to understand what Caroline was saying when she said it, how hard it would be to complete those *must-do* chores when your world has collapsed and fallen on you. Caroline watched it happen. Watched Mom compartmentalize. But on death-day I wanted my mom. I wanted her mothering to unlock my flash-frozen heart. I couldn't get there by myself.

Now, after she has died, years have passed, Caroline has clued me in, and I've chatted with death and his aftershocks as an adult, I understand the trap Mom was in.

But my cold, cold heart wouldn't thaw for years.

****

At the sudden surprise meeting about Dad's funeral, Mom was confusing, hinting we wouldn't want to be there. She was wrong. I didn't know what a funeral was, but if it had to do with Dad and if she was going to go, I wanted to go too, and I wanted us to go together as a family.

Caroline and I observed each other and saw the same sad story in each other's eyes. And we both lied and said we didn't want to go. It was the way we were trained. Mary Win didn't object.

****

A quarter-century later Mom tried to broach the subject. She wanted to apologize. The occasion was auspicious, a visit to me, my wife, and our one-year-old first-born—a peace-making visit on the adults' parts.

49

Yet the piece of my heart she needed to reach wasn't available. It wasn't the tiniest bit thawed, not ready to forgive her for steering her children away from the funeral, or for letting my dirty face keep me away from Dad on his last day.

But it was the custom back then not to have children at the funeral. Most of the funerals were open-casket and her friends thought we would freak out. Mary Win's response was more unpredictable than yours or mine. And if Mary Win couldn't go we needed to stay with her.

Caroline saw more of life than I did.

****

Post funeral, post the parade of friends and aunts and uncles and cousins from Michigan who made it south, and post everybody leaving, a quiet sickness set in. Mary Win seemed unchanged, but probably wasn't; Caroline and I became quieter and more uncertain of ourselves; and Mom completely lost it in a grief so deep it was going to tear us apart.

I can't do this, she wailed. *I want to be with your father. I miss him so much. I don't know what to do.* Whole days crying, worrying about how we were going to survive with no insurance and no money, and trying to sleep. *I can't sleep. I doze off for a second and I wake up and he's gone, and I can't get back to sleep, and I don't know what to do.*

Caroline and I heard it all. Mary Win hid in her room and in her swing, but school was out for me and Caroline, and all we could think of was trying to rescue Mom. It was our job. And slowly it gets gauzy in both our minds.

At some point Mom's talk about rejoining Dad became alarming and we didn't know what to do. She was going to kill herself, we were almost sure.

Before we could come up with a plan, it was on us.

Every morning we checked on her and made sure she got up. Until

50

the day she didn't move. We couldn't feel a pulse or see a breath. She only lay there pale. We shook her and nothing happened. Caroline, through her tears, told me she would call the grown-up next door, Mr. Watson. He came right over, told us to leave the room, kept us alone with our fears too long, and finally came out and told us she was OK. We left Mary Win out of it. Mom had taken an overdose of over-the-counter sleep aids. They weren't fatal.

That same summer, Ronnie and his family moved away and our beloved family dog died. It all ached like hell.

6. Kelley, the Y, and Me

Someone to Watch Over Me

Kelley came by the house the day after Dad died. He was our coach at the Y and the one adult the advice columnists always think exists, but usually doesn't. The one you can go to when you don't trust anyone else.

A home visit was special.

We examined the tomatoes I'd been growing in the side yard. I'd broken the ground, hauled in the chicken manure, bought the plants, staked them up, bound the plants to the stakes with soft rags, and watered them. I thought they were beautiful, and I didn't like tomatoes.

Kelley handed me the paper he'd been cradling in his big paw. It had a large, gold, round, pointy-edged sticker holding down red and blue ribbons, and written on the paper was my name in his neat handwriting for boys. Plus his congratulations for participating in the Y's spring gardening program, and his signature. Suitable for framing.

That was unexpected and cool, but the true treasure was that he'd come by to see my garden while I was there. I don't think it was an accident he came by that particular day.

We didn't talk about Dad and dying. It was enough being around him. Like a number of White boys around town, I would have a surrogate dad I could turn to, if I needed to.

I should have made better use of the option.

****

53

His full name was Cobern Frazer Kelley. A veteran of both the Coca Cola Company as a truck-man and WWII as a submariner. He could spin stories about either one, or out of the Bible, or about his canoe trip down uncharted Amazon waters. Even the Bible ones held our otherwise limited attention. (But I remember the submarine tales best.)

Race and Religion

There were no Black kids in the Y, but there were some Jews. I didn't notice the missing Black kids. Or notice the presence of the Jews. I had only two friends I knew were Jewish. I didn't know about any other religions, had no Black friends, and had no Black kids in my school. Being in White groups assumed to be Christian was my world.

****

The Jewish friend I was closest to said, *From my side it worked the same way, only in reverse. Me and the other Jews were also used to being in crowds we assumed to be Christian. We went with the flow for the most part.*

About Bible study he added that it didn't bother them or their parents. Neither he nor I ever heard anybody at the Y going for somebody Jewish because they were non-believers. Steve says that once on the Barrow School playground he was jumped by two boys and pounded for his Jewishness, but those two were always jumping somebody. True, and kid fights weren't uncommon, but Steve might have been minimizing the impact too.

Graceful in Two Dimensions

Big as he was, a little over six feet and about 180, Kelley could be surprisingly graceful. I caught sight of it first in the Y's tiny swimming pool. He climbed on the diving board, took three steps, hurdled himself up into the air and down onto the board. The board deflected, and rebounding threw him almost straight up into the air, where he casually let his feet rise over his head until he could reach up for his toes, touch them gently, straighten slowly back out, and not so much slide as sliver into the water headfirst, creating barely a ripple.

However, the most graceful I ever saw him had nothing to do with sports or athletic ability. He was the most eligible bachelor in Athens, and the grown-ups knew several women who had made unsuccessful plays for him. They presumed, probably quite rightly, that there were more they didn't know about. There was one who was most persistent.

Daughter of a prominent family, she might not have been quite there mentally. The old 1972 country song *Delta Dawn* brings her to mind whenever I hear it.

She's forty-one and her daddy still calls her baby
All the folks around Brownsville say she's crazy.
'Cause she walks downtown with a suitcase in her hand
Lookin' for a mysterious dark-haired man.

She didn't have a suitcase and Kelley didn't have much hair, but the emotional content of the song matches what I saw.

When our afternoon at the Y was done and we spilled out into the little sandlot of a playground with the kid-eating jungle gyms and monkey bars, Miss Rosemary would drive up and angle-park her car beside the chaos like any other mother. But she wasn't looking for a kid to pick up.

Sometimes she managed to find a slot right next to Kelley's sharp Buick hardtop wagon. If Kelley was nearby, he made a point of coming over to her car, in front of God, all those mothers, and us little urchins, and making five minutes of polite, gentle, gracious conversation, standing outside her driver's-side window. When he was done he would wave goodbye and go on about his business.

That was grace. As beautifully modeled as any man could do for small boys, or anyone else.

Ukulele

Free ukulele lessons!

Amounting to musical torture for anyone with an ear. But I was not so gifted, and was therefore delighted. Kelley was giving evening uke lessons.

I hunted up my old plastic ukulele buried in our attic with Caroline's E-Z Bake oven and the Howdy Doody marionette hopelessly strangled by his own strings. I brought the uke down to the Y with me and Kelley tuned it up so I could gleefully learn three chords, and I strummed along as if I knew what I was doing. Playing my three chords more or less randomly. But losing track of where it was, I sat on it. There wasn't enough glue in the world to put it back together.

We didn't have enough money to replace it, I thought, but Mom thought different. She dragged me to Durden's Music store downtown and made a big production out of choosing the right instrument for her precious son. I knew exactly what I wanted, a Harmony ukulele with a sunburst finish and white binding. The uke most of the other boys had. (My busted toy had been the only plastic one with colored strings, and I was too young to appreciate its cool factor.)

Mom insisted on listening to every uke in the store. She had a reputation for being as tone-deaf as I was (though how being tone-deaf fits with her learning to play the piano by ear I never figured out), but she was dead serious about this ukulele.

I wanted to walk right out of the store with my Harmony uke and start wailing away on it. *Ain't she sweet, just a-walkin' down the street....* She wanted the perfect instrument. I wanted to be like the other kids. I was on the verge of tears again, I was so frustrated. Embarrassed too. Helicopter-mothered before the term was invented.

She finally bought a uke sounding exactly like the others, but costing twelve bucks, half again as much as the Harmony. I didn't think we had money to throw away. I kept the uke and managed to say thank you to her. But I never liked it much.

I was supposed to love it, but she'd ruined the whole dang thing.

Blue Birds

Kelley was a builder, and not only of boys' character. He built the bunkhouse and the cook shack and the chapel at Pine Tops. And he could cook, although that got interesting on the long bus trips to Canada and California. White bread mayo and pineapple sandwiches, creamed tuna on white bread with grasshoppers, leaves, and yellowjackets chopped in for extra protein and roughage. But honest eggs and bacon for breakfast.

He could drive a bus, an old stick-shift Blue Bird or a new stick-shift Blue Bird. The two of them coexisted peacefully for a while, till the older one died. With an excess of imagination, we called them both Blue Bird.

Either bus could have driven to Pine Tops by memory, but there was a tight left-hand bend once you got onto the Pine Tops Camp Road which might have been difficult. The Oconee River was on the right.

We went out to the camp often. Overnights. Two-week-long summer sessions. Weekend work parties. But, a sudden swerve toward the river and squeals jumped out of our diaphragms. Kelley shouted over us. *No steering!* More squeals from us. On the edge of the pavement Kelley yanked the bus away from the muddy waters. And we cheered in relief.

Every single time we went out.

Class Clowns and How to Deal with Them

The cast of characters, a year before Ronnie came or Dad died: there's me, and Stan, and Roy. A lot of the time we're together, sleeping over at each other's houses, running around the neighborhood for the sheer joy of shirts-off running, playing ball in the vacant lot close to Roy's house, or inventing bicycle polo with croquet mallets and balls.

And there's Bubbie, who lives near the clay cave where we were digging clay the day before Dad died. Bubbie can shoot the lights out of a basketball hoop and is the fastest kid we know. And there's a raft of about fifty other boys, in the same grade, but from every direction in town except the Black neighborhoods.

And there's also the class clown, Andy, and his sidekick Pickett. Andy is the goof-off in class with his eyelids turned inside out. He's got a little mean streak in him, too, so he'll bully you if he thinks he can get a laugh out of somebody for doing it. Pickett is almost always around to fill the toady role.

Nobody knows how it happens, but the whole bunch of us always know where to go for Bible study at the Y, which also is the time when we get told what teams are playing each other and where. This day we're in a strange little room with a low ceiling, big concrete risers, and one dirty window that's grade-level with the playground.

We're gathered there waiting for Kelley to come in. And he does, so we quiet down. Except for Andy and Pickett and the few kids around them. The rest of us can hear a little buzz and a little snickering back there, but Kelley's up front now, and it's time to be paying attention. Kelley waits a brief second, and the room gets quieter, except now those of us halfway up the strange risers can hear Andy whisper-singing.

Lulu had a steamboat; steamboat had a bell.
Lulu went to heaven; steamboat went to hell–
Lo Operator; give me number nine.
If you do not do it, I'll kick your behind . . .

And Kelley spouts grown-up talk. He doesn't do it often. He doesn't talk down to us. He talks to us like we're people. *Andy, do you want to share that with all of us?*

But Andy doesn't back down. He says *Yes, sir.* And Kelley says, *Well, come down here and share it.*

Andy still doesn't back down. He smirks to us, his assembled multitude, and clambers down the risers to the front with Kelley and proceeds to sing. He's outfoxed Kelley. Kelley's invited him down to share, so what can Kelley do about it?

Lulu had a steamboat; steamboat had a bell.
Lulu went to heaven; steamboat went to hell–
Lo Operator; give me number nine.
If you do not do it, I'll kick your behind
The 'frigerator there was a piece of glass;
Nellie slipped and fell there, And cut her little ass–
–sk me no questions, And I'll tell you no lies.

There is silence in the room, but we're looking around at each other. We're not to use bad language at the Y, or anywhere for that matter.

We wait to see what Kelley would do. Though the song played with bad words it didn't actually say them. We didn't know the word *imply* yet, but we understood implications. Kids often do. And Andy had gotten an implied *Get out of Jail Free* card on two counts: talking when he should have been quiet, and using dirty language.

Instead, Kelley simply said, *Bend over, Andy. And Pickett, come on down here and bend over, too.*

And he paddled both of them, bare-handed. All Y-boys who got paddled became members of the unofficial *Red-Bottom Club*. Andy and Pickett were already members. It was a feature of life with Kelley at the Y, but its meetings didn't happen often. The paddling didn't hurt anything but pride, but the club's mere existence was a silent reinforcement of good behavior. Especially important for brains which sometimes took a leave of absence. A certain rock fight comes to mind.

Most grown-ups would have struggled with what to do when Andy sprang his little trap. But Kelley was way ahead. He wasn't playing Andy's game. Kelley was doing what was right.

At least that's how I saw it, and as we broke up to go play our games I didn't hear Andy or Pickett or anyone else complaining about what happened. None of us seemed to spend any time pondering the ethics of the situation. Andy and Pickett were up to their usual tricks, and they got caught and punished. Wasn't the first time, wouldn't be the last. Nothing special.

****

But not being special is exactly what made it special. Kelley understood us, little boy-kids, our need to bump up against rules and manners and see what breaks, and then to get on with life. He made behavior simple and clear, and he didn't hold grudges, push guilt, or manipulate.

And we responded better for him than for anyone else, since he made it easy. Parents didn't understand how he did it. I've never thought of a better way to explain Kelley's hold over us than this example. He made it simple.

Living Legend

I threw my pillow out Blue Bird's window in downtown Washington, D.C.

A pillow fight on a Y trip to Canada, three or four of us, and in the pitched battle I lost my grip and the pillow went sailing out the bus window.

As it left my hands I was praying it wouldn't fit through. In those old buses the windows went only halfway down. But no salvation there. The pillow went through. As soon as it cleared the window the blood drained from my head.

It became quiet in the bus a noticeable second before getting loud. I heard my name being shouted around. But I heard Kelley's voice over the commotion, and the bus quietened again. *Come up here, Jimmy.*

I did it, but I don't know how.

The bus kept going. We were in traffic. My pillow was gone. I was gonna have to spend the rest of the trip with lumpy old clothes for a pillow. Kelley was gonna be mad. I had done bad. It was an accident, but there was no way I could pull it back. I had done what I had done. My feet were lead. My head was empty and full and racing and dreading and there wasn't any place to go hide.

No place to go but to the front of the bus.

****

I got up there and fixed my gaze on my treacherous leaden feet. How did they move me all the way up there?

Did you throw that pillow out of the bus? Kelley glanced at me.

Yes sir, I didn't mean to. Almost crying, definitely mumbling.

Come see me when we stop.

I couldn't move. Now my feet would not move. *Go on back to your seat now.*

61

I shambled downcast back to my seat, every boy's eyes on me. Me still lightheaded, still frightened, still miserable. Dread is a physically sickening form of anticipation. I was ill.

And so I joined the Red Bottom Club. (The rock fight came later, in a moment of empty-headed abandon.) When the bus stopped I hung around Kelley for a while, but dealing with me didn't seem to be on his mind. I wandered off exploring the night's camping spot. Almost, but not quite, able to ignore the free-falling elevator feeling in my guts.

Maybe he's decided to let it go, I hoped. But he hadn't. I heard him ask some boys where I was and they started shouting for me. The thrill of the chase in their voices.

Now it appeared I had forgotten about coming to see him. I lost any good-boy points I thought I had. I thought of myself as a good boy, maybe too good. Now I wasn't.

My feet again got me there and Kelley said *Bend over*. And I did. And he spanked me, one good *whop* with his hand. And that was the end of it. I was now a member.

****

I walked away, and to my complete astonishment, Joe handed me my pillow.

Joe was a wordless guy, not a grown-up but not a teenager either, driving the gear pickup behind the bus. He was a mystery to us. We hardly ever saw him and didn't know anything about him, but there he was handing me my pillow. Now I seriously wanted to cry, but I held it back and thanked him.

I still don't know how he stopped the pickup, got out and rescued my pillow from the traffic. There wasn't a tire tread on it. If I had needed to, I could cry into my pillow that night. But I didn't. It passed.

****

Now I understand a little better. Punishment didn't work the way it would in the movies or a young adult book, but it could have. I could have learned *we all make mistakes, nobody's perfect,* and *it's not the end of the world* when you fall down.

Kelley's approach made it possible. He didn't dislike me for what I'd done. I didn't go on any kind of bad-list. He didn't operate like that. It was over and done and life moved on. Like with Ronnie and Jo. But it was going to be years before I understood that, and it's still not my first response to my mistakes.

Kelley's approach, his confidence and faith, and the rare ability to es-tablish boundaries but not be challenged when somebody's child stepped over his line (on purpose or accidentally) — his intuitive understanding of kids — was clearly a big part of why so many Athenians held him as a living legend.

Times Change

Things we did as young boys, and how Kelley and the Y operated:

We swam without swimsuits. Almost everywhere. Including Slip-pery Rock in North Georgia's Tallulah Gorge, where the double-decker tourist trap on the rim had pay-for-view mounted binoculars. Including when other people were already down in the gorge at the rock. One pair of college couples heard us coming and were pulling on their clothes as we got there. They eased off upstream as we stripped down.

On a trip to Deerfoot Falls, in the same neck of the woods, we hiked to the creek above the falls, stripped off our clothes and waded seemingly miles downstream to the falls, resembling strange travelogue footage of a pale Amazonian tribe. Deerfoot Falls was one of those back-country falls where, with some effort and daring, you can slip behind the torrent into a narrow niche and have your breath sucked away by the rush and chill of the water. We hiked back up the creek the same simple way, picked up our clothes and headed back to the bus.

That same Deerfoot Falls trip we boys found, and Kelley killed, three copperheads right where we were going to sleep. I'd never seen Kelley like that, before or after. He liked snakes. But he jumped at those snakes as if he hated them and beat them to death with a stick. He was quick, violent, merciless, and angry-looking. We got sticks, too, and went to sleep with our sticks in our hands, our army surplus wool sleeping bags tucked tight around us, and a wary eye which didn't last much beyond *Taps*. Be not afraid. Think biblical, not Daniel and lions, but boys and snakes in the den.

Back at Pine Tops we competed to see who got to sleep beside Kelley in the bunkhouse. When we were in our PJs, one or two kids would get to snuggle next to him while he read us all a bedtime story from *Birdlife in Wington*. Next came lights-out. We'd sing *Taps*. And we'd fall asleep. The lucky ones still next to Kelley. In the middle of the night he'd wake those of us who wanted him to, and lead us to the bathroom. I never saw what a kind way it was to help potential bedwetters with their problems.

One night he took a picture of me sleeping with my thumb stuck blissfully in my mouth. I liked the picture. I liked the idea of him watching over me in the night. But I had been trying for a year to stop thumb-sucking. Every night I'd stick my hand beneath my pillow and vow to keep it there. Sometimes I put my softball glove on, but in the night my hand would slither its way out, and my thumb would pop itself right back in my mouth. Somehow having the picture helped, or knowing somebody was shepherding me through the night helped, and by the next year I had stopped.

On the road we made our trips with only Kelley, or sometimes Kelley and Joe. Thirty or more of us crammed into Blue Bird. And Joe was the only backup I ever knew him to use, except his faith—and his belief that older boys would keep an eye out for younger boys.

Kelley worked with girls, too. Not nearly as many, and not regularly, but the few who had the privilege have never forgotten it. They were our cheerleaders, and they rooted us on when visiting teams came to town or when we went away for games. And Kelley never did things half-way—the girls weren't limited to cheerleading.

He took the girls out to Pine Tops for overnights, took them snake-hunting and canoeing, and gave them every bit of what he gave to us boys. A friend of one of the parents worried about this. Reportedly the girl's father mildly replied, *I couldn't put her in finer hands if God himself were taking her camping.*

He was unmarried. This was different in our world seventy-plus years ago. Unmarried men of Kelley's age were usually suspect. Of what, I didn't know, but grown-ups projected an uneasiness about them. Now I understand about homophobia and its corrosive effects. At the time, it didn't matter to me. It was merely another weirdness of grown-ups, and I don't think they worried about Kelley. They knew Kelley had promised God he was going to dedicate his life to helping grow boys into men. And, surprising today, it was not a con.

He never laid that *promise to God* on us. Many grown-ups I knew at the time could not have resisted the urge to play a God-card manipula-tively, but he had no need to do so. I think adults needed to have a reason for Kelley being the way he was. We didn't care. Only as we got older would we think about it.

Revised Non-Standard Version

In the legend of Kelley, his promise to God was made during a nighttime rubber-boat reconnaissance mission off his submarine in WWII. The mission and the submariners' lives were threatened by a too-close—slip into the ditch and listen to the bootsteps by your head—encounter with a Japanese shore patrol. *Dear God, get me out of this and I will devote my life to working with boys.*

It may be true that Kelley promised God, but I don't particularly like that story. I find it diminishing rather than enhancing.

I like my narrative better.

He worked with boys because he wanted to. It wasn't a sacrifice. It was his true calling. He did it because he loved doing it, and it was fun. Fun for him and for his boys and girls.

And for many of us, important.

Good Thoughts

At the Y we kept Good Thought notebooks. Many of us have at least a few pages left today, hanging around somewhere. Every week Kelley would give us a stenciled sheet on colored paper with little sayings and stories.

Mighty oaks from little acorns grow. Temper is a valuable possession; don't lose it! Dated, quaint, and simplistic now, but there are a lot of boys from Athens who remember them. Whether we apply them is another question.

One year Kelley gave us a test on our Good Thought notebooks. This was distinctly unusual. We were boys of action, and for many of us the Y was a respite from school. I generally liked school, so I didn't mind studying my notebook. I was sure I could get a hundred, and I liked doing well at stuff like that.

Come the day of the test I was excited and ready. It was multiple choice, one hundred questions, one point apiece, and I cruised through it like a seal through water. Only one question bothered me a little.

85. Put yourself _____.

a. First

b. Second

c. Third

d. Fourth

I knew this. Put God first, others second, yourself third.

But what if there was somebody or something else? You should always be last. I didn't think Kelley would have a trick question, so if fourth was an option it had to be the answer. Third was sort of a placeholder for last. Answer *d* it was.

So I proudly turned my paper in and went for a swim. You may have guessed, but I didn't have a clue.

Next week we got our tests back. NINETY-NINE! What'd I miss? Question eighty-five of course. The answer was "Third." It didn't matter if "Fourth" was laster. I was crushed. Andy, ANDY! got a hundred!

Years later, a social worker friend—who knew me pretty well, and leaned toward the idea that my tendency to sacrifice for others was pathological—said when she heard the story, *That's diagnostic.*

7. This Boy's Life

Trying

In the cyclone following Dad's death, Mom's own grief was so ferocious she hardly noticed ours, while we couldn't avoid hers.

Although she worried about us and fretted about how we were doing, she was unable to help, and her hand-wringing only made us stomp our feelings deeper. We didn't dare add to her problems, afraid one little mistake on our part would push her over the edge and she'd find a way to join Dad at last.

Caroline and I tried futilely to help. We massaged her back, gave her little presents, made her roses out of tissue paper and perfume. Nothing worked.

The day I found her crying at her desk, at the new job she couldn't hold, I was beyond dismay. I knew there was nothing I could do that would work, but I had to try. I wanted to give up, like she wanted to. But I couldn't. I didn't know how not to try.

Eat Up

Dinner during this time could be a miserable affair. Not much was said. I tried to cheer Mom and Caroline up—had no clue what to do with Mary Win—and wasn't noticeably successful at anything I attempted. Mom stayed in a funk, but did manage to keep us fed.

We ate around a small, expanded metal outdoor table squeezed into our tiny kitchen. The dining room with its formal table and lace tablecloth was too empty without Dad. It made the loss sharp as a shard.

One night, enjoying the questionable delight of *Chef Boyardee* canned ravioli, Mom seemed to have trouble looking at us. She kept trying to say something but breaking off before anything actually came out.

This made us fidgety and nervous, and we stared down at our pasta. Finally she blurted out *I'm going away for a while.* And started to cry.

Caroline and I were stunned. Mary Win seemed upset.

Caroline spit words out. *Where? Why? When? What happens to us?* Our words were jumping over each other. Followed by near-silence, a big emptiness except for Mom's crying, Caroline's crying, my crying, and Mary Win's crying. Nobody had any comfort to give anyone else.

Mom couldn't say it, but Caroline and I figured it out. Neither one of us had wanted to admit the possibility, since saying it aloud might make it true, but what else could be going on? *Mom's crazy. She's going to the looney bin* — Milledgeville, the state insane asylum which haunted a dark creepy spot in every Athens kid's subconscious.

We didn't know the half of it. Politicians and reporters knew it as a snakepit warehouse for human beings. And Mom was going there. We didn't know for how long; we didn't know if she was ever coming back; and we didn't know what they would do to her. And we begged her again, *What about us? What happens to us?*

We knew she wasn't acting right, but she was better than nothing. *Couldn't somebody help her here in Athens? Where we would go? Could we take care of ourselves and Mary Win too?*

We were frightened. Scared as rabbits hiding near hounds. In the face of our fear she pulled herself together enough to squeegee out *Aunt Ellen will stay with you for a while, and then Aunt Bel and Uncle Charley will be here and stay till I get back.* Honorary Aunt Ellen was a neighbor who lived across the street. Aunt Bel and Uncle Charley were our

70

favorite pair of Michigan relatives. Didn't matter. We weren't mollified. We were demolished.

The next day, out of the blue I heard I was going to Pine Tops. For the whole summer. I'd only gone for two weeks before. But going longer was fine with me. For Caroline it wasn't.

I was deserted. You got to go off to camp and I was all alone with Mary Win and Aunt Bel and Uncle Charley. We hadn't seen them in years. I wanted you here with me. We needed to be together.

I understand her feeling. When she married and set up house with her husband I felt abandoned too. But for me—wandering in the nuclear desert of death's fallout—forgetting the whole mess and spending the summer with Kelley and the Y boys seemed like a blessing.

I no longer cared. I was getting out.

Reliability Check

Caroline let my dereliction slide, and instead she chased my certainty. *Is that how we found out Mom was going away?*

In truth my memories of the period from Dad's death until Mom came home from treatment are covered by layers of gauze. So are Caroline's.

I remember dismal meals and awkward moments around the little metal table, eating boil-in-the-bag easy meals, more *Chef Boyardee*, and grocery store pizzas, but I can't be sure about that moment when we learned she was going away.

Caroline thinks her going away was triggered by something she did to me. I have a vague feeling Caroline's right, a sense I remembered something once, but that I've lost it. Neither one of us has the chronology of her going or her coming back. The following story of her picking me up from camp is solid but I can't be certain it happened the day she came back.

71

The Pick-up

Camp Pine Tops' two-week sessions—I stayed for four of them that summer—always ended on a Saturday before lunch. I hadn't worried about Mom, Caroline, or Mary Win the whole time. Now it was time to pay up.

Kelley told me Mom was going to get me. I didn't know she was back. The first group of parents were already arriving as we left the cook shack. No Mom. A few hours later the other boys were gone. No Mom. I started to cry. Kelley made homemade peach ice-cream, and I cranked the old-style freezer. No tears.

Kelley and I kicked around together cleaning out the bunkhouse, and lunchtime came. No Mom. BLT sandwiches. I would eat tomatoes for Kelley's BLT, but for no one else in the world.

After lunch, no Mom. I started to cry again. Kelley told me to sit and wait in front of the cook shack with my sleeping bag and my laundry bag full of dirty clothes. He'd handled enough homesick boys to know there's often a point where there's nothing else to do but leave them alone with the lost-kid blues. But I wished he could distract me somehow.

The river was right there on the far edge of the parking lot, and there were rocks to throw. So, as if my mound of bags was a magic totem, I wore a trail across the parking lot going from the bags to the river and back for the next hour, checking the muddy water, finding sticks and stones, throwing sticks and stones into the water, making sure my bags were still there, and hoping Mom had come.

It was well into the afternoon when the Olds finally did show. And I was one mixed-up kid. *How could she be late? How could she be so late?* I didn't want to look at her. I had been scared she wasn't ever going to come, and I was so mad she did come. *Couldn't I stay with Kelley forever?* and I was so confused by the feelings and the unwritten rule we didn't get mad in our family, I was paralyzed.

I looked at Mom, and she was crying. *She* was crying. I was abandoned and forgotten and *she* was crying. And I started crying too. My
world was a mess. *And why did she go away at all, if she was going to come
back and forget about me, and then cry about it?*

I think she tried to explain, but maybe she never did. It wouldn't have
mattered. My ears were going to be shut to her for a long time.

Reunion

I'm sure there was a dramatic moment when Mom and I got back to the
house. That there was a reunion celebration of happiness as what was left
of the family rejoiced in being together again. But I don't remember it.
It's lost in the gauze-fog.

I do know this much. Sometime soon after Mom and I rejoined my
sisters, Caroline and I got a feeble sense of what happened to Mom. She
had not gone to the looney bin, although the emotional impact on us was
the same as if she had. She had been at another state institution.

Mom gave us this much and little more: *Mrs. Bougerie—Johnny's
mother—suggested I go there and helped me work it out with Dr. Harry. She
knew how sad I was and called me up to talk about it. Going there had helped
her. She had been sad and weary the same way, and Dr. Harry had recommended going to the teaching hospital in Augusta. He knew one of the doctors
there. I was in a semi-private room on a special separate floor but I think I
was treated somewhere else in the hospital. They used electroshock therapy, and
a lot of it I don't remember. But I'm better now, right?*

We mumbled *Yes*, but we weren't sure yet. Knowing about the electroshock therapy scared us once we heard about it. We didn't know what
it was, but it sounded terrible. Like electrocution. Like they had fried
her brain.

Which would explain a feature of *Returned Mom* that unnerved us.

She didn't remember Aunt Ellen staying with us when she first went away. She didn't remember whether it was Aunt Bel or Aunt Dee who made the long stay with Caroline and Mary Win. She didn't remember that Bobo, the dog, had been captured by the dog catcher and died from a disease he caught at the pound. She didn't remember that Ronnie's dad had gotten a federal job and the family had moved away.

Given what we heard from Returned Mom, and what was hard to ignore about her memory, we figured they had deep-fried holes through her brain and there was no telling what had leaked out. She was back, and she cried less, but she seemed lost and like she was leaning on us for support, rather than the other way around.

And trying to make sense of our world, factoring in that no grown-ups wanted to talk about any of this, we concluded we weren't safe yet. And that we, like the grown-ups, shouldn't talk about any of it.

It was something to be forgotten if possible, at least submerged. But, of course, we never forgot, and it wasn't submerged. It's always been quite near the surface. We simply tried to keep a dish over the top.

The New Business Model

A surprise. She'd made a friend at the booby-hatch. And the friend was coming to stay with us for a while.

I wanted no part of this. But Mom saw it as the wave of the future. Like many other widow-ladies in town, she could rent out rooms in the house to make some money. And our first paying guest was to be a friend of hers from the funny farm.

Mrs. Milton was a loud, large, unhandsome woman about Mom's age. I was already set against her because she was going to be a constant reminder of where Mom had been. When she arrived she tried to be pleasant, but she couldn't penetrate my armor. To me, she was an unending irritant.

It didn't help her cause that I didn't make the adjustment to living with a stranger in the house easily. And it especially didn't help that she and Mom shared something in common—their experience at the hospital—which they were unable or unwilling to share with me and Caroline and Mary Win. As if we weren't closed off from each other enough, having a stranger who knew more about Mom's absence than we did was hard to bear.

The renter only stayed one academic quarter—she was trying to do something at the university—which was fine with me. I think Mom kept up a straggling correspondence with her for a while, but her ghost ultimately faded away completely.

Not so, the idea of renting rooms out. Renting-out was a money-maker, and we needed that. Consequently, for quite a while to come we were going to be in the rooming-house business. Which meant Caroline and I were going to be moving around the house some, giving up our rooms for paying guests. We didn't like it, but Mom's air of panic about money diminished and made being roomless worth it. Mainly.

Little by little we adjusted to Mom's memory gaps, to using different rooms, to life with strangers and without Dad, and to getting by without as much money. Mom's crying jags diminished from tropical storms to mountain showers, and she found a job with a family friend who ran a small independent insurance agency. Eventually my old passions reignited.

How to Form a Pocket

Near the corner of Broad Street and College Avenue in Athens, down from both the Varsity (hot dog joint and traditional meeting place) and the University Arch (and coincidently also close to Mom's brief and ill-fated university office), Tuck's shoe shop had the best smells in town.

Of course the whole downtown freshened up when Benson's Bakery's production line was in full swing, but that sweet aroma was only baking bread. The shoe shop smelled of raw leather and boot-black, a sharp, tangy mixture of work and skill and textures and oiled machinery, complemented by the *ssh, ssh, sshing* of the constantly turning overhead wheels at the cobblers' benches.

This, in the late '50s, was back in the day when shoes were repaired, re-heeled, re-soled, patched, stretched, polished, and dyed. We got our leather bootlaces there at the shoe shop — not at the grocery store — cut from leather hides right there in the store and hung from hooks above the bench you sat on while you waited or tried on your fixed-up shoes. The bootlaces weren't only for boots though, they also worked for suturing over-worn baseball gloves, and the neatsfoot oil you found at Tuck's softened stiff new mitts as well as boots.

Forming a pocket in a new baseball glove was a secret art requiring a can of neatsfoot oil, an old baseball, a lot of sweat and pounding, plus the knowledge, passed down from boy to boy for generations, of how to center the pocket below the webbing but not too close to the heel, and why it mattered.

In light of that, my mom never knew what grief she caused me by not ever having been a boy. To her a ball-glove was a ball-glove, like a basketball was a basketball, and a football was a football. As a result the sporting goods I got from her were the JC Higgins line out of the big Sears wish-book, and none of them were worth a darn. The basketball was silly light and rubbery, bouncing insanely high off even the soft grass in the backyard. The football was a squashed version of the basketball, but with white stripes around its now pointy ends.

And my glove. My mitt came at a horrible instant in time where the totally flat hand-glove-like mitts of the '20s and '30s — nothing but padded rags made from leather — were about to fade into oblivion but hadn't quite cleared the more clueless stores and catalogue outfits. Those

76

emporiums would include Sears and its hapless JC Higgins line of cut-rate, second-rate sporting goods, made, I think, expressly for widows to give to their unfortunate sons. Who else would buy them?

I tried to form a pocket into the shapeless five-fingered monstrosity. I tried neatsfoot oil, 3-in-one oil, motor oil, vegetable oil, every oil I could get my little thieving hands on, and nothing worked. I wrapped said glove around old baseballs so tight it squeaked. I put it under my pillow so the weight of my head would smush it into shape while I slept. I jumped up and down on it to loosen it up. I was reduced to beating it with the baseball bat—a broken, shattered one I'd salvaged and tacked, glued, and taped back together. When the beating didn't work, I put the abomination out under the tires of the Oldsmobile so Mom would run over it—with both tires I hoped. I tried every suggestion offered by every other boy I played with.

And with all that it was as worthless as the day I opened up the box and pretended to be overjoyed.

My Heroes Have Always Been Cowboys

Playing ball wasn't the only passion reignited following Mom's return from her adventures in 1950s mental health treatment. I went back to my interrupted love affair with Lash LaRue.

A cowboy idol of screen and TV and small-town fandom shows, Lash subdued bad guys with an eighteen-foot bullwhip. Lash wore guns, but seldom used them. Dressed in black, he was the epitome of cowboy cool.

I myself had two sharp pistol rigs. One was a two-gun Roy Rogers set-up with the holsters riveted in place to the belt, so it had limited abilities for adjustment in attitude—sort of like old Roy's acting. The other was a Hopalong Cassidy outfit and, while Hoppy had less star power, his rig could be set up for cross-draw, one gun or two, without having to buckle your belt on backwards. Or sling one gun low off your hip and tie it to your leg, to be mean and dangerous. I loved Roy the cowboy better—he was a Sunday night family ritual when Dad was alive—but Hoppy had the better guns.

However, since my hero, Lash LaRue used a whip, I needed a whip. I needed one badly.

But I wouldn't pray for one. Somewhere in Sunday School I'd learned it wasn't good to pray about such little concerns. If victory in a Little League game was too picayune a want to pray for, a bullwhip was definitely not going to get a response. Or at least not a good one.

There was a distinct possibility that God might not approve of bullwhips for little boys, though he did let his own son have one to work over the money-changers at the temple.

I was good at saving my money, which would come in handy if I found a whip to buy. I got a little allowance from Mom and seven cents for each football program I sold at the university football games. If that wouldn't do it, Mom was a sucker for my passions.

I think she had a guilty feeling about Dad's death and how it left his boy fatherless. (Though the truth was she fought hard for him. It was Mom who found the article suggesting *Rauwolfia* might be the miracle discovery Dad needed, but it was too late.) And Mom overcompensated for not knowing beans about how to raise boys.

So if I wanted a bullwhip to complete my cowboy life, she would make sure I got one, whether it made sense moneywise to her or not. Since we were poor (by our standards), this lack of financial smarts on her part troubled me some, but I didn't always restrain myself.

On the other hand, with my experiences with her baseball mitt, football, and basketball choices, I knew I couldn't let her choose a whip for me. The bigger problem was I had no idea where you went to get a good bullwhip.

78

It never occurred to me to ask for help with this question. I think it is the inevitable fate of being a kid to hate relying on other people for your needs, but, after my parents' failures by death and falling apart, lack of trust became ingrained in me. If I couldn't figure it out, it wasn't figured out. This did not serve me well later on, but seemed my only choice as a kid.

So I wasn't going to get a bullwhip. I didn't know where to look. I didn't want to ask. And if I did want to ask, I didn't know who to ask. (*Excuse me Pastor, where do you think I might find a good bullwhip to purchase?*) No, I don't think so.

I could live with that. I could watch Lash and Roy and Hoppy on the TV, one of Dad's legacies to us, and I had not only both two-gun set-ups, but boots, spurs, cuffs, shirt, vest, hat, and a trick lasso with a swivel eye.

All in all, I was pretty well set up in the cowboy line. It was a little sad not being able to be Lash LaRue, but, like I said, I could live with it.

A New Glove

I put the whip out of my mind and returned to the five-fingered monstrosity problem. Maybe it was time for me to buy a new glove myself. A block north of the shoe shop and most of a block west, down from the Holman Hotel, Mr. Williams ran the world's best sporting goods store.

This is where I made my great leap forward. I started studying new gloves with a seriousness of purpose. It had its upside (a possibly nice new glove) and its downside (if it didn't work out I couldn't blame Mom). Surprisingly, I had no guilt about leaving Mom's gift behind. Maybe I'd paid my dues long enough.

In baseball season Mr. Williams stocked the front part of his store and his small display windows with outstanding gloves—gloves major leaguers could wear. I couldn't afford those, but I loved trying them on.

Most were way big for me, but I still loved the feel. New, out of the box, they were too stiff to play with, but they had pre-formed pockets, and intricate web designs. I knew what one of those mitts could be, because one day at recess Harvey Westbrook let me use his glove during our ritual after-lunch game. His was a hand-me-down Rawlings, but it didn't have hand-me-down stigma. It had history. His uncle was a minor league player and this glove had seen and played with guys who made it to the Bigs. The mitt was too big, but so well broken in small-handed me could flex it and make miraculous catches. It was magic.

Now, if you weren't playing in the Bigs or the Minors, the secrets to making a glove flexible quickly were akin to the secrets of forming a pocket: lots of oil, neatsfoot preferably; but instead of the wrapping and pounding for pocket forming, it was — surprise! — lots of flexing.

Oil the hinge up, keep the glove with you, and keep sticking it on your glove-hand and opening and shutting it relentlessly. You didn't need a ball in it, because the pocket was already there. On the other hand, if you were older, and skilled and lucky enough to be playing in front of crowds, your glove got enough action in a season to get flexible, or worn out, on its own.

Obviously, my new glove wouldn't get broken in on its own, so I was going to follow the recipe, but I was going to add what I thought was my own innovation to this ritual. I planned to oil the thumb joint of the glove, too, and make it so flexible you could squeeze the glove till the pinkie and thumb met.

But I'm getting ahead of myself. Back at Mr. Williams's store I was so sick of the five-fingered monstrosity I picked a four-fingered glove instead. No one else I knew had one, but it fit my small hand perfectly, and had a deep manufactured pocket and E-Z flex hinge built right in. It was made by Spalding so I knew it would be good, and sure, it wasn't a Rawlings, but it was one I could afford.

I spent a lot of time in Mr. Williams' store, regarding his goods, picking them up and testing them. But I didn't spend a lot of money there. He never frowned or looked cross at me or urged me out the door. He didn't seem to mind at all. It was the only place I would ever think of to buy a glove.

So, I paid Mr. Williams, and thanked him, too. But ran out the door with my new best friend still in the box. Hustling the two blocks down to the shoe shop for a full can of neatsfoot oil. When I walked in, my jaw fell down and my eyebrows leapt up to the top of my forehead.

On the far-left peg, where the thirty-inch bootlaces should be, was what seemed to be a brand-new, untreated, not quite finished, braided, golden leather six-foot bullwhip. When I got my breath, I hurried up to the counter and asked Mr. Tuck, who wasn't as friendly as Mr. Williams, if the whip was for sale.

He said *Eight bucks.* A heap of money. I'd already paid thirteen dollars for the Spalding glove and I didn't have another eight dollars. I had about a buck and a quarter left which was enough to get the neatsfoot oil, but not much else. When I paid for the oil, I asked Mr. Tuck if he would hold the whip till I came back with the money, and he asked *When?*

I didn't know when. It wasn't football season so I couldn't earn the money at the next Saturday game. My allowance was only a dollar a week, and money was tight in the family. We didn't get paid for chores, so I couldn't hustle up a bunch of work. I could earn another dollar a week delivering grocery fliers door to door. So the quickest I could promise was four weeks.

Fuh-four weeks? I stammered. A shy kid anyway, pressure situations like this made me want to merge with the old wooden floor under my feet.

Mr. Tuck said *No. I'm not gonna hold a nice, new whip for four weeks. Somebody else could walk in anytime, like you did. Tell you what I'll do though. You get your momma to call me tomorrow and I'll hold it till the day after.*

81

Thank you, Mr. Tuck. I'll ask Mom to call. Not what I wanted to do at all. But appearing to be the only choice I had. I took my can of neatsfoot oil, stuck it in the box with the Spalding, and left the store.

I needed to think. We were too poor for me to be asking to spend upwards of twenty-one dollars on two purchases of nothing but toys, both in the space of three days. It didn't matter if some of it was my own money. I knew it wasn't right. But I craved that whip. I couldn't imagine anyone else getting it.

✻✻✻✻

Oh! Suddenly I could. I remembered the other fevered kids at my cowboy birthday parties. Any one of them would love to have a whip, and I hated them for that. What if one them walked in with a mom who had ready cash? There were more of them than me, and all of them were better off.

The store door behind me opened, and I didn't want to turn around.

You Can't Always Get What You Want, But . . .

The shoe store door closed, and a lady I didn't know walked over to the counter and asked Mr. Tuck if her shoes were ready. No kid in tow. No glancing at the bullwhip. No asking about its price.

I had lucked out. I was downtown anyway, and Mom worked in the Southern Mutual building just a block up College Avenue from where I was standing. Since I was nearby and it was quitting time I thought I'd run up there to see Mom and ask her what to do (against my code, and a sign I had already panicked).

I had to be careful, though. My eyes hadn't toughened-up yet, still revealing what I thought was unmanly sensitivity. I did not want to start crying in front of Mrs. Abney or Mom. Not talking about the whip until we got out of the office seemed like my best move.

I'd show Mom and Mrs. Abney the glove and tell them how nice Mr. Williams was, and leave it there until Mom and I were in the car headed home. Operating in my *figure it out myself mode* I couldn't think any further ahead.

And that's how it went, but when we got out of the building, I couldn't contain myself anymore and I blurted it out in a torrent.

Mom, guess what? Mr. Tuck's got a bullwhip in the shoe shop and it's for sale, and it's only eight bucks, but what am I going to do because I spent my money on my new glove, and he won't hold it for me for four weeks, and I can't get eight bucks in less than four weeks and somebody else is going to get it, and he won't probably ever get another one — it's the first one I've ever seen there, and nobody else has one, and I really want it, and will you call him, please? I knew it! I was in tears by the time I got the flood of words out.

Immediately I started to back out of it. Mom remained quickly distressed, more easily raining tears than before our loss. (I was tougher, I thought, and I cried too easily.) And she still talked about going to be with Dad, which scared us a lot. I didn't want to put any more stress on her and our precarious finances, although I wanted the whip badly.

Mom I can live without the whip. You probably think it's dangerous. And maybe he won't sell it until I can pay for it. And of course, I started to cry again (so much for toughness). I hated that.

She surprised me. Sometimes she did that. She got cross. *He's got a lot of nerve not trusting you. We've done business with him since we came to town, and he's seen you since you were born. If you say you're going to do something you do it. And he should know that if you didn't make it right, I'd do something about it.* She paused.

He's not closed yet. You go right back in there and tell him you want the whip put on layaway and you'll pay him two dollars a week until he's got his eight bucks, and that's what your momma told you to tell him.

I hated that. I was not fierce. I could stand up for myself on the playground OK, but it seemed I always wound up crying about it and being led up to the teacher by the girls to tell what happened. I hated that too.

So that's how I wound up with a bullwhip and a new glove. And no, I didn't march in like a little soldier with God on his side. Nor did I get through it without tearing up some more. But I stammered it out. Mr. Tuck agreed, and oh how I loved the glove and the bullwhip. Our family finances didn't fall further apart, and unlike some of my passions, my fire for both the whip and the glove lasted.

The confrontation I hated, and I still avoid it, but I think now Mom was right to make me do it. Sometimes it has to be done. The Rolling Stones said it best. *You can't always get what you want, but if you try sometimes, well you just might find, you get what you need.*

And sometimes, rarely, you get both.

My Baby Loves the Western Movies

There were four movie theaters in Athens during the '50s — the height of my cowboy infatuation. One of them doesn't matter because it was on its last legs by the time I had my ninth birthday, and the other three each had different rules for Black people and White people.

The Palace, home of the Saturday morning Kiddie Club, where you could get in for ten cents or Benson's Bread wrappers, didn't let Blacks in. And, as far as I knew, the Harlem didn't let Whites in. So that was fair. The Georgia, however, let both races in, only the Blacks had to enter around on the side and go straight up to the balcony.

I prized going to the Westerns at the theaters. I loved getting the popcorn and Coke at the refreshment stand and agonizing over the choice of candy to go with it. I was so busy with my world I never wondered while I was at the Georgia if the Black people in the balcony could get refreshments. And I don't remember there being two sets of bathrooms. What did they do? They couldn't use our bathrooms.

The management kept us so apart I don't think I ever ran into a Black person there. Or, more likely, the invisibility of Black people to White people blinded me. As an adult, I can't imagine any movie palace giving up profits from the concession stand, regardless of the need to keep the races separate.

I knew a little of the mechanics of segregation by then, the White and colored bathrooms and water fountains, the janitors and maids always Black, people in charge always White, White boys not expected to open doors for Black ladies, but I didn't understand it as a system, much less question it.

When you're a White kid it's easy to be ignorant. It won't kill you. The world is the way it is and that's just the way it is. Georgia in the summer isn't sweating hot and humid; it's only summer and you're out of school. Fall isn't a pile of color-coordinated tree-discards and temperate temperatures; it's the time to play football in your shirtsleeves. Blacks and Whites keep separate, and that, too, is just the way the world is.

However, only an anti-cowboy numbskull could be blind to one kind of discrimination shown by the theaters. For some reason unfathomable to me, the Ritz, the Palace, and the Georgia conspired not to show Lash's films. It's not like they didn't show Westerns, they simply discriminated against Lash. Maybe the operators didn't like whips. I never knew. Despite my love of cowboy pictures and my love of Lash LaRue in particular, I never saw a Lash LaRue movie.

But, in one of the strangest moments of my kid-life, I did come close, and could have seen him in person while I was at it.

It happened like this. I had come in from the backyard, dressed in cowboy gear and sweating from a hard practice with the bullwhip. I had mastered the overhand crack, where you bring the whip back over your shoulder by raising your arm and rolling your wrist back, then complete a quick double-pump forward-back wrist snap, sending the working-end of the whip, the popper, through the sound barrier. A hugely satisfying kinetic sound experience.

Next, I started working on a variation of the overhand crack. I was trying to swing the whip around my head like a lasso and suddenly reverse it to snap the whip. It took more effort and coordination than I thought it should, and it wasn't going well. I headed into the kitchen for a milk break.

Beulah Mae was there on the screen porch ironing and I went to talk with her while I drank my milk, straight from the glass bottle delivered in the morning. She'd given up on reminding me not to drink out of the bottle, and I'd forgotten it wasn't ever the right way, hurry or no hurry.

The movie situation was nibbling at my mind. *Beulah Mae, how come they never show any Lash LaRue pictures in this town?*

Only half listening, she started to nod her head as if she understood, but stopped in mid-motion, gawking at me like I was mouthing Esperanto.

No really, Beulah Mae, I see the picture-show ads every week and they never show Lash. They show Roy Rogers and Gene Autry, but they never show Lash LaRue. How come?

She stopped eyeballing me funny and startled me through my bones.

The Harlem shows Lash LaRue pictures all the time. He's coming in person next week.

I reeled. *Beulah Mae, don't be teasing me about this, please. It's not funny.*

No sir. I'm serious. This is the first time he's come in person, but my boys have seen his pictures. They're like you, they love the man with the bullwhip. People say he looks a lot like Humphrey Bogart.

I didn't care about Humphrey Bogart. I was jumping up and down with the milk bottle in my hand, about to slosh the milk out of the bottle.

Are you sure? How come he goes to the colored theater but he doesn't come to the Georgia or the Palace?

I wasn't aware enough to feel bad about saying "colored," or to understand the racism of what I was saying. In my world, as I understood it, White people always got the best of everything and they always got it first.

Beulah Mae's revelation that Lash would be at the Harlem was a fundamental shaking of the order of the universe.

Ignoring the order-shaking and foundation-crumbling, I sputtered, *Besides, I can't go to the Harlem even if he is there. They don't let White people in.*

They do too, she snapped. *They can sit in the balcony, just like colored folks do at the Georgia.*

****

My world fell apart. I didn't yet know the word *irony*, but here was a photo-negative image of the Georgia Theater and the whole White world, going on almost in my neighborhood, and I didn't know anything about it. How could this be?

I was too stunned to talk anymore. I put the milk back in the refrigerator, picked up my whip off the kitchen counter, and went back outside. Uncoiling the whip, I snapped off an underhand crack, but my heart wasn't in it.

This was an impossibility. This was a hugeness beyond impossible. Lash LaRue at the *Harlem*. Another kid would have asked Beulah Mae to go with him, to show him how to behave. But this would violate the boundaries of our kid/maid relationship. Would I pay for both of us? How would we get there? If we went together where would we sit? Could we sit together? Or would she sit on the main floor, while I sat in the balcony? Would there be other White Lash fans, or would I be alone? Could I get popcorn and Coke and candy in the colored theater? Did they have refreshments? Could I go to the bathroom? Was there a side entrance for me?

None of my friends had told me Whites could go to the Harlem. Did Mom know? Would she let me go? Would I go with friends? Could I go with friends? Would their moms let them go?

A kid less determined to solve his own problems would have asked Beulah Mae these questions or asked his mom. Me, I couldn't figure it out on my own. I couldn't begin to figure it out on my own. The immensity of the opportunity and its challenges to the world as I knew it totally overwhelmed me. For once I didn't cry. I simply gave up. I put it out of my mind.

I never saw a Lash Larue picture, and I never saw Lash in person. And I never told a soul about it until I was a grown man with kids of my own.

But, to this day, my whip hangs close to hand.

Existentialism for the Very Young

Caroline and I had dropped into a pit of uncertainty. Self-confidence was in the past. Being bereaved, financially strapped, and hitched to an uncertain mother did that to us. The swiss cheese holes in Mom's memory would remind us of the family's provisional status every time they appeared. And any time she cried we got nervous.

We tried not to let it show.

There was shock when we understood we were swimming in sewage. The sewage overflowing and landing on the good and bad alike. Our first brush with existentialism. And there was a growing sense we were almost on our own. Mom could come through sometimes—thank you bullwhip, for the lesson—but it wasn't a sure bet.

Wasn't some folkwise older person supposed to step in and help us kids out?

I read ahead to a seventh-grade story collection my folks had to help Mary Win with her reading. It was filled with stories like that, and stories about young kids who had to grow up quick and do super strong and brave things. But I didn't know what it was I was supposed to do, or how to do it.

Bouncing up and down as I was in a strange new teeter-totter life, I recognized yet another oddity throwing the balance off.

How come if we were poor now, we still had help?

The kind that in the South meant Black people working for you.

The Help

I was flustered about having a yard-boy (our White term for a Black man of any age who did residential outdoor work). Eugene, who worked on and off part-time for us, was an actual boy. I focused my fretting on Eugene because of that.

Since we were both boys and he wasn't much older than me—and because it seemed like he was doing work I could do—it seemed wrong for us to hire him. I was trying to figure out how to be poor.

It's not that I wanted to do more yardwork, but I thought I should. Or get an after-school or summer job. *I was ten, I was supposed to be the man of the family, I was supposed to take care of Mom. Shouldn't I be doing something more?* These *shoulds* didn't wear me down, but I could hear them in my head whenever he was around.

I didn't resent him for it, though. I actually liked him. He was strong, cool-looking, and friendly. Unfairly, I let my resentment fall on Mom. It seemed to me she should have asked me to do more. But if she had, I probably wouldn't have done a good job. She couldn't win.

And gazing back I can see reasons why she wouldn't ask. Caroline and I were already doing chores, and we both picked up jobs when we could. Mom might well have been trying to protect us from feeling poor.

In the heavy yardwork there was another possibility. She, like most people, would probably rather work in tandem with someone who wanted a job and worked effectively and enthusiastically than with a whiny kid who only thought he should be doing the work, didn't enjoy it, and wouldn't follow directions well.

Because Mom, in a rare bit of non-conformity, worked right alongside Eugene. This probably scandalized any White person who happened to see it, since a White (middle-class) lady wasn't supposed to sweat, or work alongside a servant, or—*Heaven Forbid!*—sweat alongside the help. I think her passion for her garden and hard physical work blinded her to the fact no other White woman was working together with her Black yard-boy.

For the guilt problem only I knew I was having, there was also an untried solution. If Eugene had asked me to help him, I'd have done it in a flash, and done it well. A teenager asking me to help? I'd have responded like a good, well-trained dog.

****

Beulah Mae was an institution. She'd always been around, and the stuff she was doing wasn't boy's work, in my opinion. The ironing, dusting, window washing, floor polishing, cooking, serving, sweeping, vacuuming she did—I didn't like any of it. I doubt she did either.

But because I didn't think it was boys' work, I didn't worry about one of us picking it up to replace her and make the finances easier. I did ask Caroline about Beulah Mae though, when I started picking these issues apart. Why did we keep her on? There was a simple answer.

I think Mom was worried about Mary Win being alone all day if we were at school and she was at work.

That makes sense to me.

So, we got childcare and housework at the same time.

90

****

In addition to hired help, we had gentle, steady support from the community. Fresh garden vegetables left on our doorstep. Credit, and a job for me delivering flyers, from the grocer—though we were always a little behind. Gently-used hand-me-downs to wear, from what seemed like everyone with kids older or bigger than we were. Wonderfully mysterious deposits into Mom's bank account. A new bike for me one Christmas from the Kiwanis club. Glasses and—more generous yet—contact lenses from the Lions. Braces from Rotary.

I wasn't grown up enough or hadn't been poor long enough to honestly appreciate the hand-me-downs, but I wore them. Including, since the clothes kept coming in, to my first high school homecoming dance a few years later.

Like a puppy in a clothes closet, Athens' generosity chewed away at the *poor-me* cloak I was planning to wear.

Long After I Left

When I started rethinking my childhood, a question returned—*How come if we were poor, we still had help?* But I posed it differently. *If we were poor, what were they?* If we were scared about losing the house, what about Eugene and Beulah Mae? Were they struggling too? Maybe struggling more?

At first, I assumed they had to be worse off. But my mind was running in the same ruts it ran in when I was at junior high.

I assumed that because they were Black, and only because they were Black, they had to be poorer than I was. I hadn't yet fathomed there were income differences in the Black community as well as in the White. But at least I could grasp the truth peeking in my window. An awful lot of people had less money and town help than we did.

91

It's possible neither Eugene's family nor Beulah Mae's was as well-off as we were—before Dad died or after. But it's also possible they were as middle-class as we had been, and I couldn't see it because they were Black.

How Poor Were We?

Every month Mom would sit down with the bills at the big dining table and ask me which ones we should pay. She'd open her big blue spiral bound business checkbook, a holdover from her secretarial training, show me the balance in the bank, and show me the slip of paper with the bills and the total. *Who do you think we ought to pay first? How much? All of it?*

It was like a jigsaw puzzle, trying to fit the money people wanted from us into the amount of money we had. We could never pay each of them completely in a month, and some months one bill might get nothing except a note from Mom, *I'll catch up the next month. Mrs. Donald J. Weddell.* We always made sure to pay that one in-full the next month up, but somebody else might wind up not getting paid anything. We rolled the privilege around. I favored paying the people I knew best first.

****

Dad, in the recorded annals of Dad (not many), only made one mistake. It was a doozy. His lack of life insurance wasn't it. High blood pressure made him uninsurable. His lack of Social Security wasn't it. Georgia didn't accept it until 1956. (Family lore has it Dad voted for the safety net on his deathbed, but died before the votes were counted and it passed.)

Dad's mistake was writing his will without a lawyer.

I, Donald James Weddell, being of sound mind and body, do hereby bequeath my entire estate to my wife Winifred Tornblom Weddell [This is where he should have stopped.] *in trust for our children, Mary Winona, Caroline Elizabeth, and James Douglas Weddell.*

One simple sentence. What could go wrong?

The lawyer reading the will said Mom couldn't dispose of any assets. The last phrase *in trust for our children* meant, he said, *The assets are not yours Win, they belong to Mary Win, Caroline, and Jimmy. To sell anything, you need to get a Guardian appointed by the courts for your three kids. It might get complicated because Mary Win will require a separate Guardian due to her mental handicaps. In which case the two Guardians might disagree.* Mom threw up her hands, politely, and said she'd think on it.

She waited till we were out of the office to ask. *Do y'all think we ought to do this? Go to court and get court-appointed Guardians?* Breaking the silence that followed, Caroline piped up. *Nobody cares about this except us. We don't need to do anything. We've got to live, let's keep doing what we've been doing.* Mom sighed in relief, *OK, let's go home.*

The bank owned the house, the Oldsmobile could hardly be considered an asset, the miniscule teacher's retirement pension Dad left behind couldn't be sold, and we needed it for cash-flow anyway. So, there was no need to chase the Guardianships idea down the rat hole.

A few years later, Mom should have gotten a genius grant. From out of the blue, or, for her, maybe from God, came an understanding. We did have an asset. We merely hadn't recognized it.

Dad's tree farm, a ratty old piece of third- or fourth-growth pineland in the neighboring county, bordered by dirt roads and worn-out cotton ground gone to weeds. The tree farm could be an asset.

None of us doubted her. Anything hopeful she said was a blessing in and of itself.

I didn't think the farm was big, but I was caught up in the excitement. We hadn't had anything promising in a long time. Everybody brightened up.

When we had gone there with Dad, a bit of a car trek into the country itself, first we'd pull the Olds off the road, then hop out and spread the picnic. When we were done eating, Dad and Caroline and I would shoot his twenty-two at cans set in the road bank.

All of us except Dad stayed close to the road we came in on. He would wander into the scrub forest, machete in hand once the shooting was done. Mom and Mary Win stayed near the car, unless Mom wanted to straggle off and chase Dad, in which case Caroline and I would stay near Mary Win. Sometimes the three of us would go over to airplane rock or house rock and play one of our made-up games.

When Mom came back, Caroline and I might venture a little deeper into the trees, but not far. When Dad came back from his timber cruising, we'd eat whatever was left in the picnic basket, pack up, and head home.

Those memories were comforting, but we never went out anymore. It would be too far to go to be too sad when we got there.

Yes, sell the farm. Paying some token obedience to the lawyer, Mom asked us if she should sell Dad's tree farm. We were still short every month. Mrs. Abney's job didn't pay much. There was nothing on the horizon. *Yes, (please) sell the tree farm.*

The farm was bigger than I thought, a hundred acres. Mom asked one of Dad's forestry friends to sell it for us. He got a hundred dollars an acre for it from a pulp-mill company. Ten thousand dollars in 1950s money. Enough to pay off the house and have a small cushion in the bank.

We weren't poor anymore.

The Knife

I spent a lot of time in the shop where I bought my glove. In my head I saw a sign lit up in bright red neon, saying,

MISTER WILLIAMS SPORTING GOODS
THE BEST IN ATHENS!
(KIDS WELCOME).

The Kids Welcome part flashed magnificently.

Mr. Williams had everything I ever wanted (except a missing parent) shoehorned into his narrow little slot of a store. In addition to the competitive sports gear, he carried rifles and shotguns too.

Including a beautiful little Remington pump twenty-two weighing barely enough to seem like a genuine gun and seeming to be a new part of you when you nestled it to your shoulder. Mr. Williams didn't flinch when you re-racked the Remington to pick up a Browning twenty-gauge over-and-under shotgun. It shouldered as well as the Remington, but was far prettier, with an engraved receiver, checkered pistol-grip, walnut stock, and tiny recoil pad.

The store made me grin every time I walked in, because it held yet more. In the back were bikes and in back of those, a bike repair shop. Plus, every Christmas Mr. Williams had Lionel trains and the Lionel train catalogue. And always a knife case.

****

Nowadays every little two-bit convenience store and filling station has a knife case, but in those days the only one I had ever seen was in Mr. Williams's store. He had a Swiss army knife—when they were rare. He had a humongous Bowie knife. He had beautiful pocketknives—one blade, two blades, small, medium, large—and right in the middle of the case, displayed like a jewel, was a knife like no other I've seen to this day.

This knife had only one possible purpose, a purpose obvious to anyone from the teardrop blade-shape alone, let alone the two finely honed edges and smooth flat red handle. This was a throwing knife. It wasn't for carving or whittling, gutting a deer, or stabbing people. It was for the sheer sinful pleasure of throwing something sharp which would stick where you threw it.

Boys are not supposed to have such pleasures. I knew that, Mr. Williams knew that. Every sane mother on God's green earth knew that. A boy could be told with a different knife or a hatchet to use it right or lose it. What could you possibly tell a boy with a throwing knife? *Don't throw it?*

There could be only one point to having a knife so enticing in a display case. To make somebody want what they couldn't have. Not only was I sure I shouldn't have it, I was in the same position I had been in with the bullwhip. It wasn't football program season, and I didn't have the cash. Sorely tempted, I wouldn't take money out of my tiny savings account for something so forbidden.

****

The knife cost fifteen dollars. It would cost me eight weekly trips with grocery flyers to every door in my neighborhood, the next neighborhood up to Five Points, and back to the high school plus most of my allowance for the same eight weeks.

Fifteen dollars was a large amount of money. More than my glove cost. The most money I'd ever spent on anything. And a lot for something with no useful purpose. Only good for one thing. Throwing.

I wanted the knife like I had wanted my bullwhip.

And I cut the time down to six weeks, doubling up on grocery flyer routes and collecting coke bottle empties for the two-cent redemption.

But I was a responsible kid — sometimes.

I should ask Mom first before I bought it, though I thought of it as my money. Suppose we needed the money for something else. Buying the knife was an extravagance. And we weren't extravagant. And besides,

I had heard those grown-up admonitions about knives, and knew a boy my age shouldn't have a knife so sinister. I'd hurt myself or someone. I'd already landed a homemade dart in my sister's shoulder.

Mom said yes.

****

I couldn't believe it. The knife was as good as mine. I'd watched its beauty grow for weeks before I decided to try for it, and I spent weeks saving. In those weeks no one else had bought it or examined it carefully. (In my self-centered view, if it wasn't gone, it had to be because no one else had looked at it beyond a glance.)

I was convinced no one else knew the chrome-plated blade ran through the handle, so the handle-end was a delicate chrome and carmine sandwich. No one else knew the sandwich was held together by only two chrome rivets with the heads ground down and polished to a mirror sheen, like the blade. No one else had held it in their hands, feeling the balance, and fighting the almost irresistible urge to throw it right there in the store. No one else, except Mr. Williams, knew how much I wanted the knife.

I went to the store and bought it. Just like that, I bought it. It was mine. It was beautiful and it was mine. But I didn't feel good once I got it home.

The pleasure was gone. I threw it half-heartedly at a few trees. I wasn't any good with it. Sometimes it stuck, sometimes it didn't. I wasn't gonna get any better either. No knife-throwing circus performer was going to miraculously appear in my backyard with a beautiful assistant and teach me how to throw it right.

I didn't know what to do. I knew I wasn't supposed to have a throwing knife. No mother in her right mind, much less in our circumstances, would let her kid get a knife like that. Why couldn't she have said no, like every other mother I knew would have? Sometimes I just wanted a sign she was normal. A sign I didn't have to make the right decisions on my own.

Mr. Williams took the knife back. I was worried he wouldn't since I had thrown it some. But he did.

Fifth Grade

That year everybody in Barrow School learned about knives. Or at least switchblades. Three boys in the school bathroom, DT, Spally, and Cole. Cole had the switchblade. They weren't illegal yet. Lipstick red or jet black, deathly beautiful, their spring-loaded, push-button, snap-open action made them a boy's dream. They were also easy to find, and cheap, not expensive like Mr. Williams's throwing knife.

In the bathroom at the urinal, DT was finishing up when Spally yelled. And immediately there was a lot of excitement.

Mrs. Rosenthal's classroom was right next to the boys' room, and Spally came running in pale-faced and yelling again, *You gotta come in! You gotta come in!* He didn't look good.

Mrs. R. told us to get out our maps and work on the products of Georgia and hurried out of the room. Spally went with her, whether to try and explain or out of reflex because he knew he was in deep trouble, but their rush out the door left nothing but excitement behind. Nobody got their map out, but a huge buzz, like the angriest hornets' nest ever, burst out.

Didn't do us any good either. Nobody knew anything. Well, maybe somebody knew a little something. Brendon, who rounded out a three-some with Cole and Spally, was in our class, and the buzz got softer as a whisper started passing around. *Maybe something happened with a knife.*

A knife? What kind of knife? Whisper, mutter, murmur, squeak. *Maybe a switchblade? A switchblade!* a little louder. And then dead silence. And eyes on our desks. Mrs. R was back in the room. Without three boys.

She didn't bother to ask about the products of Georgia maps. She simply stated and commanded *There's been an accident. Now get out your math book.* She was all business, all the time.

I didn't like her. She was a big lady with gray hair and a long face with too much flesh on it. She never smiled and her eyes were always watching. Her voice had the bark of a seal which didn't go with the rounded grandmotherly shape we had seen in our fourth-grade readers. She didn't have the soft empathy either. We got out our math books.

I was lucky this happened in the afternoon. Otherwise, I'd have missed the biggest event to happen at Barrow School since the winter it got so cold they shut down all the schools. The school system being out of coal.

****

I had taken to staying home mornings, pretending to be sick. Which is why I would have missed the knifing if it had been a pre-lunch extravaganza. Mom was letting me get away with the sleeping in. Did I mention Mrs. R was boring? She had a reputation as a hard teacher, but she was mainly boring.

At recess, the story grew until it settled on a wild but believable version. Cole stabbed DT with a switchblade he brought to show off. Spally had gone to the bathroom with Cole because they were best friends and usually up to something together. The stabbing was an accident. When Spally yelled, DT whirled around and the knife went into his thigh. Cole was standing too close. Cole and Spally were in trouble. DT was at the emergency room with his mom. He wasn't in trouble with the principal but might be with his mom just because.

This fit what little information we could piece together, all of it suspect but taken as gospel. It fit the personalities so well it made sense to us. It would be days before we got the supposed true version, for some people, years. It depended on where you were in the kid network. There are still a lot of different versions out there.

****

The knifing, accidental or not, was unprecedented at Barrow. But to me personally, it was eclipsed by a simple book report.

****

In the middle of the year, Mrs. R assigned an oral book report. We had to do one. No excuses. Our choice of book.

I read a lot. And I could write book reports. What I couldn't do was stand in front of the class and read a report to the class. I don't know why it was different from show and tell, but it was. Horribly different. This was to be the second thing since Mom got back from the looney bin she insisted I do. I cried and everything. She wouldn't budge.

Worse yet, and as I knew would happen, I also cried all the way through the report. Kids were staring away or down, anywhere but at me, not to be kind, but because they were as embarrassed as I was. And I couldn't stop. Leaking salt-water from the time I got up from my desk until well into the next kid's report. I wanted to disappear. To slide down under the desk, grow into a paper-wad, and be blown into the corner behind the bookcase.

Not admitted at the time and hard to admit now, but the ordeal did start to cure me. I hated it, but my shyness did get better. I didn't think it would, but it did.

****

But in first place for the biggest, most lasting event in a memorable year—beating out the knifing and the oral report:

Mom failed my test.

I think I knew at the time what I was doing. I wanted her to be strong, and to prove it to me. By the time she made me stand up and do the book report it was too late. My test had been running its course from the start of school.

More than every other weekday I'd wake up, tell Mom I was a little sick, and ask her if I could stay home from school (tedium unmentioned). And she'd say yes, every time, and I'd stay home. But home alone with Mary Win and Beulah Mae was more boring than school. After lunch I'd walk to Barrow and rejoin the class. At first it was strange, and I thought the other kids would ask me about it. They didn't, and once it became a pattern it was merely what I did.

Here's what Mrs. Rosenthal, old eagle-eye, nothing gets past her, had to say on my quarterly report cards.

First quarter, present 28 days, absent 17: *Even though Jimmy has been absent very much, he has managed to keep up and do excellent work.*

Second quarter, present 32 days, absent 13: *Considering how much time Jimmy has missed, this is an excellent report.*

Third quarter, present 25 days, absent 20: *It's surprising how well Jimmy is able to keep up with so many absences.*

Fourth quarter I ended my stay-home strategy. Present 42 days, absent 3.

And I gave up on Mom.

****

I was going to hold my grudge forever. Mom was never going to be reliable again. Despite her firm stance on the book report and her

101

insistence I stand up to Mr. Tuck, I was sure she was never again going to tell me *No* when I needed her to. I was on my own.

The demand that I do the report was too late, too little. We'd never had the best relationship, and her not-too-long-before disappearance into crying jags and into the horror story crazy-house had scared me badly. And hurt so much I was going to do without her if I couldn't trust her. Be like a man would be—not feel anything at all.

Mom hadn't had her genius moment yet, money was squeaky tight, and maybe I was holding a grudge, but something had been wrong in our house ever since she got back from electroshocking.

They'd patched her up in South Georgia, but something got left in the ward down there. She left some of her tears and crying jags under their care, which is what everybody wanted, but she was missing something else, too. Not only the memories whose disappearance startled us time and again for a while. There was a certainty to her character I hadn't always cared for, but which I sorely missed now she was back without it.

Caroline and I, and probably Mary Win too, were still scared, and no one ever talked about any of it. We desperately wanted our old family back, or at least something like it. Maybe I'm projecting, but who could tell how the others truly felt, with all the nothing being shown?

Between Mom and Mrs. R., at least I wouldn't be quite so shy.

Moonlighting

At home, despite the age and gender differences between Caroline and me, and my increasing reluctance to open up to anybody, there were parts of our lives we shared closely. Like visiting Mom at her new job.

The last year we were still at Barrow together, 1959, Mom got on at the university with better pay and benefits than Mrs. Abney could provide. Mrs. Abney had actually encouraged Mom to keep trying for a better job. She understood our situation. We owned the house now, but every month we nibbled away at the tree-farm-sale leftover.

Barrow wasn't far from Mom's new job on campus and Caroline and I could walk over after school and visit her at work, do our homework there, and ride home with her. I remember those walks and visits as joyous outings. We were relieved to have Mom doing better financially and mentally. She was crying a lot less, and our seeing her being successful buoyed us like helium in a weather balloon. Putting it less positively, those visits helped us work loose some knotted insecurities.

Mom had been hired to organize a small branch library serving one of the ag college schools, whose library had previously been on a self-serve honor system. Caroline and I wondered whether she was hired because they truly needed someone, or because they sort of needed someone and Mom definitely needed a better job.

The fix was in. The dean of that school had been Dad's best friend and was technically our guardian. (Not court-appointed but picked by Mom when the will-lawyer said, *Georgia law requires widows to have a Guardian for any minor children.*)

While Mom was regarded as a great secretary—her misadventure in coping on-the-job while grieving raw somehow hadn't diminished her reputation—she had absolutely no library training. But personnel systems were less systematic and more pliable in the '50s. I silently mistrusted how she got the job, but I knew.

It was our relationship with the dean. And while the job made a remarkable difference in our lives, we were undoubtedly the beneficiaries of something inherently unjust. There had to be more qualified people around the university campus. But I'm grateful. It's one of the big ways the town cared for us.

My relief in our reinforced footings far outweighed my small sense of unfair play. I kept those thoughts to myself. (And, for the record, I wasn't thinking about the Whites-only context of university employment for anything above a menial level.)

Mom's clearing the hurdles allowed the whole family to breathe easier. So, after school, if we didn't have something else to do, we'd like as not walk on over to visit Mom, and if the dean was in, we'd go visit him too. Mom pretty much insisted on it.

Mom loved the job. Loved the students. And particularly loved the IBM Selectric typewriter which came with the office equipment. She was typing letter-perfect theses and dissertations on a stiff old manual upright Royal at home, still trying to make enough to pay the bills when they were due without dipping into the bank account. It wore her out.

****

After a few months settling in at the job, Mom started going back to her library in the evenings. Rather than fight the old Royal at home she'd use the Selectric at the university. But the loud, elegant, busy professional office floor by day turned deserted and cavernous at night. With the building's twelve-foot ceilings, terrazzo floors, reduced fluorescent night lighting, and deep shadows, the night sounds transmogrified into echoes sounding too much like somebody else's footsteps.

After a few nights alone with the spookiness, Mom asked me, Caroline, and Mary Win to come with her. The first time we did it, Caroline and I understood immediately why we were there. It was different from the bustling, peopled place we visited in the day. The four of us were merely dust in the emptiness.

Caroline and I quickly get tired of being quiet ourselves, of doing our homework, and we'd start rambling, leaving Mary Win with her Bible, her pretend class-record book, and her paper dolls sitting near Mom. We'd explore, first nearby, then a little further off, then down the hall to the empty dean's office. Then we'd run back, like a rubber band at the limit of its elasticity. It didn't feel safe too far from Mom, so we'd snap right back.

Mom did well at the job and passed her probationary period, so we were safe, by our standards. It wasn't quite enough financially, but it was more, and the benefits helped. Over time, Mom worked her way up to a better-paying secretarial position in the same building. She'd organized the library and left it in good shape for a qualified librarian. Now she had a job she had competed for fairly (except, of course, for the Whites-only rigging), and which paid enough to cover the bills. Slowly we crawled ourselves up to the lip of the hole we had been in. Close enough that Mom was able to buy the now out-of-date Selectric when the school surplussed it and bring it home.

Caroline and I still visited in the daytime, but nobody had to go back there at night.

Secret Heard Later

About our daytime trips to the dean's office:

When Caroline visited the dean once by herself—I was at the Y—he asked her to sit on his lap, kissed her, and stuck his tongue in her mouth. She ran back to Mom but didn't tell her. Or me, until Caroline and I were both in our fifties.

The Dean. Dad's best friend. Our guardian.

I had wondered why she would never go down to his office without me after our first couple of visits. Now I know.

Letting a Person Know

I wanted to go to the Y's other, non-Pine Tops, summer camp—Big

Y—and the way Mom and Dad and Kelley raised me, I was going to have to tell Kelley. Telling Kelley made sense to me at the time, and still does. However, it wasn't easy to do.

I thought going to Big Y was breaking faith, or turning my back, or making a mistake, somehow doing something not quite right. And it must have been wrong somehow, because I couldn't tell anyone the actual reason I wanted to leave Pine Tops and go to Big Y Camp. Big Y gave out awards and Pine Tops didn't.

I wanted one of those awards. Not the ones like archery ranks and riflery ratings. I wanted the *Best Camper* award. An emblem, like a high school letter, for being the best camper in your age group. The Athens paper even wrote you up on the front page.

I could already feel the pride of wearing the Y emblem. It was sort of sickly, the pride I hadn't earned yet, because it was tied to a sticky sense of betrayal and loss.

But it would sound conceited and stupid if I told anyone. You can't tell people you want to be a big-shot somehow, to be special and have everybody know it, and have something to prove it. It was vain and needy at the same time.

It didn't feel good, but I was going to ask Kelley if I could go.

His office wasn't big. A big, flat-topped, scarred oak desk, a swiveling barrel-backed oak desk chair, two floor-to-ceiling bookcases with books and photographs and mimeographed sheets hanging over the shelf-edges, and two doors. That was it. There wasn't a second chair. Boy conversations weren't long, and there wasn't room anyway.

Kelley was at his desk. Wasn't much place else he could be in his office, and I walked up and asked, *Kelley, can I talk to you?* I was standing; he was sitting; and I had to look up at him. He was big. *Sure, what do you want to talk about?*

I'd like to go to Big Y next summer. There it was. I couldn't make it go away. I'd turned my back on Kelley. At least that's how it seemed to me.

106

Was there something in the way he regarded me? Was he disappointed? Surprised? I couldn't tell. I was sure there must have been something, but I wasn't reliable in fraught situations.

There was a reason I asked Kelley before I'd talked to Mom. It shows in my reaction to Kelley. Lots of boys made the change I was winding myself up about, but I was conditioned.

If I'd asked Mom about the switch beforehand, she'd have asked me all sorts of questions, *Why? Are you sure you want to quit Pine Tops? What's better about Big Y?* By the time she finished I wouldn't have been sure of what I wanted.

I was looking at Kelley the same way I would look at Mom, waiting for the axe to fall.

Too late it occurred to me Big Y would cost more money than Pine Tops. Money which wasn't lying around anywhere in our house.

And Kelley said, *OK. I'll talk to Pop about it.*

That was it. No questions. A simple encouraging answer, and the deal was done. Pop made sure the Y helped out by giving me a camp-job, and I went to Big Y come summer.

8. Athens High School

Letterman

First day of high school. I was so proud.

I had bought a white cardigan sweater—the billboard for high school athletic awards, and asked Mom to sew my Big Y Best Camper emblem on it. It looked great. I thought everybody would be impressed. Merely a lowly freshman, but not too cowed, I glowed with enthusiasm for being in high school and having such a neat sweater to wear on my first day.

I was still small, but I wore my camp emblem sweater with what I thought was nonchalance until Danny, a classmate, but a big kid from out in the county, saw me wearing what appeared to be a letter sweater, and did a classic double-take. It had the wrong letter. He didn't say anything. He didn't have to.

I heard it in my head. *THAT KID DIDN'T EARN A HIGH SCHOOL LETTER! HE'S A FAKE!* I turned around, walked down to my locker, took the sweater off and never wore it again. It wasn't a high school letter. It was just a small kid's small triumph.

Homecoming

A big deal at Athens High. Not that alumni came back in packs—their presence was so minimal I didn't guess their return was the purported purpose of the event. But we were frenzied about the Homecoming

Kings and Queens and their escorts, the football game, and most certainly, *the Dance.*

Freshmen frequently didn't go, but for reasons of wanting to be one of the in-crowd, I was determined not to miss my first one. Which meant not only going to the pep rally at school, to the bonfire before the game, and to the football game, but also to *the Dance.* The last one is the one which counted when we proudly said, *I'm going to Homecoming.*

I had only two problems. No clothes, and no date. One did not go to Homecoming without a date (or, of course, without clothes).

One of the families leaving vegetables on our back porch solved the clothing problem. A slightly worn, slightly out-of-date hand-me-down wool suit came along with the squash before I started to worry too much. I was embarrassed by the pleated pants. They had disappeared from the wardrobes of young people, reeking as they did of old men hanging out at the county courthouse.

In spite of the reeking, the suit was better than anything I had, with coat-sleeves much closer to where they ought to be. No Ichabod Crane gangly wrists style for me. So, I had clothes. Now came the hard part.

Finding a date. By unwritten rule, no one attended single. Still shy, I had not started dating yet, and I hadn't made any new girl friends since the first year of junior high. I had new boy friends, but not girls. Maybe one of those girls I'd known forever would go with me, if I could find the nerve to ask.

How long could I procrastinate?

****

The music at the dance would be good, from a local or regional band. Covers of pop tunes off the Top 40 charts — *Cathy's Clown, Teen Angel, The Twist, Runaway.* Maybe a sprinkling of crossover hits from the R&B list — *Finger Poppin Time, Save the Last Dance for Me, He Don't Love You*

110

(Like I Love You). If the band was Black (in 1961, segregation had relaxed enough to allow it) there would be more R&B, and the number of Black people at the party would increase to match exactly the number of band members.

Athens High was otherwise (except for the custodial and cooking staff) a White, segregated school. Civil rights actions and reactions were all over the news in the '60s. I noticed but didn't pay any mind. When the university lost a lawsuit and finally admitted Charlayne Hunter (Gault) and Hamilton Holmes, my junior high hallways had echoed the chants of the rioting White students. *Two, Four, Six, Eight, We Don't Want to Integrate!* It was news but I didn't see it affecting me. My new high school life was consumed by fitfully adjusting to low-dog status in a new school, swimming practice, and Homecoming.

Brown v. Board of Education had been decided when I was in second grade.

****

When I was about ready to stop procrastinating about asking a girl to Homecoming, I pondered who to ask. There were six or seven girls I thought I could approach, and Mary was my first choice.

We had indeed grown up together. Her folks and mine were friends. Both sets of folks were part of the ag college set doing things together, and they lived in the neighborhood. We went to the same church. When I wasn't heading down to swim practice, Mary and I would walk home from school together, and sometimes I would carry her books. Think quaint Americana, roller-skating together on her front porch when we were little. Mary's waters ran deep and still. While I covered my shyness with chatter and teasing, she was quiet, and very, very smart. I liked Mary for all of this.

It made sense to me that I could ask her and that she would be the first girl I asked. I hoped there wouldn't have to be a second one to ask. If there was the need to ask another girl, I was pretty sure my nerve would fail me. It didn't matter how long we'd known each other. This was different. This was Homecoming, and it was a *Date*. I was glad Mary said yes. And now I was truly set, with clothes *and* a date.

****

Of course, I was wrong.

I wasn't set for Homecoming. I wasn't set because Caroline wasn't set. She didn't have a date. The unwritten rule about not going single to Homecoming? It applied to upperclassmen, too, and especially to girls. At Athens High this was the kind of appropriateness most girls worried about a lot, at least as I understood it.

And it was my problem as well as Caroline's because, while the two of us had never learned to be demonstrative, we were fiercely loyal to each other. I didn't think it would be right for me to go to Homecoming if she couldn't. It wouldn't be fair.

Girls weren't asking boys out in sixties Georgia unless the school was having a special Sadie Hawkins dance, so Caroline didn't have a choice to be the one who asked, and probably wouldn't have taken it if she had. And I was sure it would be a bad idea for me to ask a boy from the school on her behalf. I didn't ask her about it, it seemed so wrong.

Had I boxed myself in, asking Mary out before Caroline's plans were set? I couldn't have waited any longer to ask someone unless I wanted to be turned down. And honestly, I hadn't seen it coming. Beginning to panic, I grasped at flotsam, *If Caroline didn't get a date I could still go with Mary, couldn't I?* Caroline would, in fact, insist, but I'd feel rotten about it.

And if I stayed home, what would I tell Mary?

****

I wrestled the Homecoming mess around for a while and got no-where. Time was disappearing, and I was beginning to feel desperate. I was doing this worrying on my own, naturally. I had learned little good came of sharing or asking advice. I hadn't told Caroline I understood the dilemma we were in.

Then I ran into a guy I'd met at the pool. We both had tiny sailing craft. His was a converted rowboat, mine basically a large surfboard with a sailing rig, daggerboard, and rudder. We sailed Lake Lanier several times, including a windy, coolish fall trip where I had spent more time in the water than on top of it.

Norm, a college freshman, told me I reminded him of his brother. A good thing, he indicated. Projecting off our sailing connection and his friendliness, I started wondering if he would like to go to a high school homecoming. At which point it seemed like I should abandon dithering for a more straightforward approach. The supply of time continued to diminish.

Unusually communicative and smart for me, I asked Caroline what she thought of the idea *before* I talked to Norm. She gave me the go-ahead and I was therefore committed. I had to do it. It took a lot more pumping myself up than I thought it would, but I made a point of running into him the next day and explained my predicament.

To my surprise, because we weren't close, he was willing. He wasn't fazed by this out-of-the-blue blind date proposition. I wondered if may-be Norm was lonely. On the other hand, maybe he liked the idea of meeting Caroline and seeing if it went anywhere. He might have been missing female companionship.

No matter how, the four of us were going to Homecoming! I bought a corsage for Mary and bravely, if shakily, pinned it on the lapel of her well-cut new fall suit. She was a pretty girl, which I sometimes forgot since we'd known each other so long. Beautiful night-sky dark hair and pale, clear face. I was proud she'd agreed to go with me.

The game would be outside in the university's Sanford Stadium, and it would be cold. Caroline would twirl batons at halftime in her form-fitting red sequin majorette costume, shivering mightily, and Norm would meet us at the dance.

I missed earning my high school letter freshman year by one point. Homecoming with Mary made up for it.

Our Paying Guests

Don't advertise and don't rent to girls. They're messier than boys.

That's what Mom learned from the widow network. *Don't advertise because advertising can trigger the integration laws* (Actually Mom's friends were ahead of the times. The Fair Housing Act wasn't passed until 1968. But they were already worried.), *and you'd have to rent to anyone who meets your qualifications. Plus, your qualifications can't exclude Black people. So, don't advertise. Let your university friends know you've got rooms for students. You'll fill up.*

And counterintuitively, the widow-ladies said, the girls are messier than the boys. Stockings and cosmetics everywhere.

So, we rented to White college boys. Mom had high hopes for the arrangement. We would rent out the upstairs with its separate bath, and there would be room for three. Two sharing the room Caroline and I had shared as little kids, and one or two in the former attic Mom had converted to a separate bedroom when Caroline got old enough to want some privacy.

That worked out well enough until we rented to a shirt-tail relative.

****

My second cousin twice removed, the only one of those I knew I had,

114

seemed younger than the students we usually got. He was still reading comic books, which was not something college students did in those times. I think he was also the only one who came to us on a family recommendation rather than through Mom's university friends.

I came home from swim practice one afternoon to find him gone and the household in a muted minor key uproar. Mom was home and pulled me aside.

Louis is gone. He made advances towards Mary Win, but she's OK. Nothing happened. She told me when I got home.

Maybe it was Mary Win's difficulties in communicating to Mom, or maybe it was Mom's Victorian prudery which kept further details from me—except this one. When it happened, Mary Win was frightened, but had enough sense and gumption to leave the house and retreat to her swing in the backyard. The twice-removed cousin left the same day. Presumably right after the incident, before any of us got home.

Mom followed up with protective measures right away. We stopped renting to male students, and we made sure Mary Win always had someone at home with her.

****

The advice Mom had been given was wrong. The girls who followed shirt-tail were nice and not messy. One of them persuaded Mary Win to give up her room, an un-imagined possibility. Caroline and I liked her too, and occasionally hid in her room and surprised her when she came home from classes.

She had a component stereo set with large speakers—the first record player of its kind we'd seen. Sometimes she'd let us play it. When she left, she gave Mom a check. Not for rent, but as a gift. Shadowed over the next few years by several others. Part of her religious practice as a Unity Church member. We were touched.

But as Mom's university jobs lit her up like a firefly, and her thesis work—typist, editor, proofreader, and advisor—continued its punctuated flow, we supposedly got out of the rooming-house business altogether.

Until Mom couldn't resist a woodlands student with recommendations from people she knew in the School of Forestry.

Time had passed but it seemed like a flip-flop. Two changes at once: renting again, and to boys. Would we be hunting for a room ourselves, like hermit crabs shuttling around for a new shell?

The would-be woodsman arrived in town shortly before university classes started, was short on cash, and hard up for a room. But he offered Mom an irresistible deal. He would waterproof the basement and paint the house in exchange for free rent in our raw, former coal chute, spider-haven basement. All he wanted, other than the basement dungeon, was a little help from me.

The basement was a scary place, strangely seductive in a sinister, secretive way. Going down the steep unprotected stairs was like being inside a horror movie, the last scene in the cellar of *The House on Haunted Hill*. Where the voice in your head is shouting *Don't do it! Don't go down there. Are you nuts?*

In wet weather there could be six inches of water over the concrete floor, with drowning camel crickets, live daddy long legs, the aforementioned spiders, and monster Georgia cockroaches (all called Rudolph by Mom, as in *Jimmy! There's a Rudolph! Kill it!*). I had to wade through the swamp to turn on the sump pump. There wasn't a pair of barn boots or galoshes in the family. I went barefoot, pants rolled up.

The sump pump was in an open, boy-sized hole in the concrete floor. I had to lean over it while stretching to reach the valve handle. (The pump wasn't electric, operating instead off the cold-water system using suction from the moving water.) Wading down there to open the valve wasn't optional, it was one of my must-do chores.

Changing out fuses when the floor was wet was stupid, but when the floor was dry it was only disconcerting, what with reaching into an electrically live box, unscrewing old, dead, glass fuses, and replacing them with good ones. Reaching through spider webs and watching for spiders. Made a kid a bit nervous.

Given those issues in the basement, getting our subterranean pest-shelter waterproofed and occupied sounded like an OK deal to me. When I learned my labor on the house painting and waterproofing had been thrown into the bargain, rather than being peeved, I liked the idea of being useful.

****

Robert the forestry student worked out well. Not only did he improve the house; he was what Mom had prayed for, someone male and older for me to look up to and emulate. Apparently, Kelley wasn't enough. Maybe she held my love of football against him.

****

I hated her good-male-influence idea. It was another way of saying I wasn't OK. My own fear inclined there already. *Am I raising myself right? Why can't I control my tears? I ought to be tougher and stronger.*

During the time we regularly rented to boys, I cried every time she made me go upstairs to visit them for some male bonding. It was so forced and awkward I reverted to the worst of my shyness. *Why did I have to go ask them? Why didn't they ask me?* She could have hinted what they should do.

And although I hated those visits, secretly I longed for something exactly like she envisioned. Though Kelley was doing his best, I was sure I was missing something significant from the male world.

****

Well, maybe what I longed for was not *exactly* like what Mom envisioned. In my indistinct yearnings, I knew one thing. *There has to be a guy way of thinking about sex I don't know. And it is different from what Mom says.*

My first clue: I was a teenager. I knew masturbation was wrong … and irresistible, it turned out. Bible said the first one. My body said the second one. Body won.

And my second clue? Mom said to watch out that some girl didn't lead me down the primrose path. She didn't explain what a primrose path was, but the way she said it made me think maybe it was what I wanted, whatever it was. But this primrose path stuff wasn't what I expected from *The Talk*. And I didn't want to get *The Talk* from Mom.

Sometimes she spoke like she was from a stilted period-piece, and her warning sounded like what her mother so terribly long ago might have said to her, substituting girl for boy. It did not sound like what I hoped Dad would have said to me.

Mom chose to tell me this primrose path pearl of wisdom in front of Caroline, in Caroline's bedroom. Was there nothing Mom understood about boys? I wasn't sure I wanted this talk from her to happen, and, if it did, I was positive I didn't want it to happen in front of my sister in her bedroom. In my adolescent boy-world, anything—motels, bedrooms, bras, car back-seats, drive-ins, laundry—could be sexually charged.

The advice column, for instance. Strangely, the advice column. Dr. George W. Crane's *The Worry Clinic.* What was the biggest problem? Sex. Whose fault was it. The woman's. What should she do? Meet her husband at the door when he came home from work. Wear a sheer, lacy nightie and welcome him home appropriately. *Whoa, Nellie! They let me read this stuff in a family newspaper?*

But Mom continued with *The Talk*. Mercifully briefly. The rest of sex-ed at home consisted entirely of her asking a shy, reticent son, still in the presence of his sister, if Kelley had told us anything about sex. I uttered a quick quiet *yes*, my sole contribution to the conversation. I took it as an exit line.

First Kiss

While I wasn't above misleading Mom, Kelley had in fact given us a great talk about the human body, complete with a plastic torso with removable organs, and he explained the mechanics of sex and the occurrence of nocturnal emissions. He got a question when he asked if there were any. It came from the slowest boy in the whole group, and maybe the bravest.

Is the little black stuff in the bed when I wake up nocturnal emissions?

No, Tim. It's not. Unspoken by Kelley, and every other boy in the room was the thought, *Tim, it's just bed gritch* (the sandy toe-jammy stuff sneaking into bed with your feet, refusing to go back onto the floor with a few hand-sweeps).

The talk by Kelley, despite its slightly squirm-inducing nature, was helpful, but didn't come close to filling the need I had for low-key, low-stakes, older-guy talk about sex, with someone I trusted. Kelley was celibate, by choice. I was determined to be, at least at some unknown later point, un-celibate, by choice.

****

That older guy I could trust turned out to be Robert. A non-traditional student, he'd done a hitch in the army right out of high school and worked for a photographer once his enlistment was up. Unlike most undergrads, he was closer to twenty-five than eighteen. From him I learned to paint houses (the most work and the secret is in the prep), to care

119

for my brushes, to love old Johnny Weissmuller Tarzan movies and the Kingston Trio, and to shoot his big Winchester twelve-gauge automatic.

He won my heart at the safety lesson when he set up a number-ten can twenty feet away, handed me the shotgun, made sure I knew to keep it pointed down-range, had me check the safety was on and the gun unloaded, gave me one shell to load, told me to aim at the can, push the safety off, and squeeze the trigger. A hugely satisfying twelve-gauge boom and the can was blown to shit (although I still wasn't using words like *shit*). I understood the point—guns are dangerous—but his no-nonsense demonstration cemented the friendship.

Now we were close enough to talk women, as well as guns. His conversations as we worked together painting the house helped with my sex ed. Mom and the church and the 1919 copy of *Sane Sex Life and Sane Sex Living* (mysteriously appearing on the family bookshelf about this time) sided together in reserving sex for marriage. Robert didn't.

He told me some of his encounters when he was younger, and made it clear he used condoms when matters went far enough. I said little, mainly listening, absorbing the attitude. There was a mutuality about sex which seemed to exist between him and his dates. An entirely new concept. I liked it.

But there was one conversation we didn't have. I couldn't start it, and Robert didn't. He might not have known quite enough about the family to know how to broach it, although he wasn't exactly shy, but I think he suspected most of what was going on. It would have made a difference if he had said something. I'd have been more secure.

Ever since Dad died and Mom got back from the hospital, she had been pointing out men to me whom she thought I should admire. They were men who were devoted to their mothers. And most of them had never married.

She went further and pushed me at them: older, white-haired, well-mannered, pale, weak-eyed men who were attentive to women in an overly polite, asexual way. This shoving was almost the same as she had done with me toward the college boys upstairs. But the college boys were young and vibrant. These older guys were mushy, and her determined nudging seemed disconnected from any sane purpose. What was I supposed to gain from this? What was she supposed to gain? Was it all for those pathetic gentlemen's benefit? I was too old to cry, but I was painfully mystified.

Once she went what should have been too far, but I did what she asked anyway. At her insistence I visited one of those doting men. He lived nearby in a daylight-basement studio apartment. The venetian blinds were closed in the daylight, and he sat on the bed in the sad light barely sneaking through the slats of the blinds.

Our conversation was brief, tortured, and like being imprisoned in dime-store pomade. I sludged through it only with great effort and emerged feeling unclean. I was being used for something, I was sure, but I didn't know what was in Mom's brain. If I'd known the term, I'd have said it was like being pimped.

****

By the time Mom had worked on me for seven years without Dad, I had gotten one message clearly: my purpose in life should be to stay home and take care of her and Mary Win.

Yet her choice of role models was bizarre. They scared me to death. They were so far from the guy she had married: dark, handsome, lively, outgoing, charming, warm, forthright Dad. How could Mom possibly want me to grow up like one of those over-sensitive momma's boys grown old? I couldn't handle this.

I backed yet further away from her.

****

I think Robert understood some of this. Understood he could make a difference for me. His sex talk was certainly refreshing. Actually more sensible, it seemed to me, than everybody else's. All he did was tell me what he'd done, and encourage me to be more adventuresome.

These stories made sex sound fun (and achievable).

****

Robert was alternating between guarding and minding the refreshment stand at his local pool. A girl came up to the stand with the straps of her one-piece hanging down the front. He tugged at them. She did the unexpected. Pulled them the rest of the way down, *So you want to see?*

And pulled the straps back up.

He got her number, called her up, and the same evening they were parked off one of the local deserted back lanes, and she was showing him the rest of her well-designed body. He did the same for her and then they merged efforts.

Robert's simple smile as he told the story is what sold it, along with the way he avoided bragging. It was more a *See, look what you can do* tone, which made it yet more enticing.

He also showed me the rip in the headliner over the backseat in his '52 Chevy. A different girl's toe had done that. With that story, he showed me where he kept his condoms in the glove box.

From a different guy, maybe with a sneer or a leer, this would have had a different impact on me, but Robert's matter-of-fact manner and his ability to tell a story let it make sense to me. It didn't solve my problems, but it helped.

I was always going to have trouble reconciling what I had been taught by church and family (and which had been deeply stained within) with what I was learning about my inner workings, but I was getting a sense you might could be a good person and not follow the sex rules as they were given.

****

I had recently begun dating. It had not gone well. There was a party with a band, lots of dancing, and opportunities to sneak off—none of which I took because I wouldn't know what to do—and a vicious hard-on which wouldn't subside, and which I also didn't know what to do with.

My next dates were with one girl in particular. We were doing movies and bowling and there was a lot less pressure. We enjoyed each other, which helped. But I hadn't gotten the nerve to kiss her. I thought it might not be unwelcome, but I didn't know how to go about it. Robert said just do it, which was the least helpful advice he ever gave to me.

Somewhere in my brain, I knew she liked me. She'd invited me to a party at her house, which gave me the courage to ask her out in the first place; but showing affection was something I did only through teasing. It was all I knew. Holding a hand, putting my arm around someone, hugging a friend, these were unused novelties in my meager communications toolbox.

It's not that there wasn't an appropriate moment for a kiss. In my culture the boy walked to the girl's front door to pick her up for a date. No honking the horn from the car. And at the end of the date, you walked the girl back to the door. And came an awkward moment (unless you were already past it), *what do you do next?*

In my case, you stood there a stupid-long time looking like I'd come up fast against an upper-cabinet door, and stuttered *Uh, uh—goodnight,* and walked back to the car thinking, *I should have kissed her. I could have kissed her. I should have kissed her. What is wrong with me?*

Finally, with Robert's continued encouragement, my own natural interest, a feeble sense it was OK and normal, and with a right arm deadened by a night of pretend physical contact (mainly with a theater seat-back) and a head full of doubts and questions—*Do I ask if I can, or do I just do it? Lips or cheek? Say goodnight first or after? Just do it, idiot!* — I kissed her.

It was not a marvelous moment, except for my pride and relief.

****

A couple of months later I heard through roundabout channels how un-marvelous it was for my date. To a girlfriend she said, *It was like kissing a board.*

****

At home, Mom seemed to be vaguely dissatisfied with my nightlife. Each girl, and there weren't many, had some flaw or other, or Mom was hoping I'd be around for a family night.

One item she was clear about, though. *Nobody's good enough for my children.* I didn't know what to do with such a comment, so I let it roll off my back. I thought it was another meaningless cliché people her age said. Maybe it was supposed to show her love for us had no bounds. The problem was, I never heard any other mother say it, and heaven knows I sat politely through my full share of old ladies' gossip and chat.

Eight years later it dawned on me—after having listened to Mom complain about Caroline's boyfriend-fiancé-husband Bill (and pretty much any other boy Caroline brought around or dated), and do the same, but at a less-fevered pitch about the girls I dated—that Mom meant it.

More years later, when she said *Nobody's good enough* to my wife Bertie, it stopped rolling off my back. I had to ask myself, *why would she say*

124

that to my wife? And where would that have left me and Caroline? Living out some spinster-siblings-and-demented-mother Southern horror story?

Catching up to the News

Athens' population exploded in the '60s (forty-one per cent increase in the decade, to 44,000 in 1970), but the city continued its small-town touch.

Many of us in school had known each other since we were born. Some of us had rolled together in baby buggies. But it being a college town, there were also always newcomers. Three of my friends, Robert, Margaret, and Hilde joined us in junior high.

Despite so many of us growing up together, or maybe because of it, we didn't talk often about big ideas. Our high school lives were day to day: school, sports, dates on the weekend, church or Mass on Sunday (Seventh Day meetings or temple on Saturday for a few), and repeat. Part-time jobs for some.

Mrs. Maxwell, our tenth-grade World History teacher, tried to open intellectual doors for us, but we were pretty slow to walk through. In 1963, the whole town was abuzz and energy was high, like it was two years before, when the university was being integrated. This year rumors were flying about the public schools being integrated too.

Unexpectedly, Mrs. Maxwell brought it out into the open, asking us—exactly as if she was asking us for an interesting fact about Kaiser Wilhelm—*What do you think about integration?*

There was a moment of silence while we watched each other, and the unspoken thought *Are we allowed to talk about this?* ran through probably everyone's head. Someone broke the quiet. *Our class is going to be integrated by a colored girl. She's the daughter of a colored doctor. That's what I've heard.*

A few kids might have known more, I had known less. It depended on how plugged into the gossip mill your parents were. But lots of kids had opinions. Few of them acceptable today.

This was not a class full of overt Klan sympathizers. It was an accelerated class, appearing and acting middle-class, and almost completely products of our Southern environment. Our public disdain for the Klan was probably more class-based, more not wanting to sound trashy, than brain-based or heart-based. Being good at school didn't necessarily have any relation to racial attitudes.

The arguments against integration were typical of the time and place. *We have our places and they have theirs, and it would be better if we kept it that way.* (Nobody went for the *Why? Why would it be better?*) *The academic level would decline.* (No high-schooler I knew cared about the school's academic level before the rumors started.) *It's not really what they want. It's just outside agitators pushing them to do it. Even if it was a good thing, which I don't think it is, we need more time to adjust.* (Mom held this opinion into the late-'70s, and probably longer. We stopped talking about it.)

Unsophisticated arguments, but we were only tenth graders. I think most of the kids were parroting what they heard at home. Only two kids expressed the unusual idea, *Integration is the right thing to do.* I didn't chime in one way or the other.

By this point, my shyness in school matters had vanished, so this was unusual. I was conflicted, and not willing to say anything about the conflict. About how I had grown up one way but was beginning to have doubts about *our* way. I knew it wasn't outside agitators causing the ruckus.

Before the discussion had time to wear ruts, Mrs. Maxwell asked for a vote. Not a secret ballot, but a show of hands. Out of the thirty (all White) kids in the room, only two had believed, or had the nerve to say, Black kids ought to be able to go to school with us. (No-one phrased it *We ought to be able to go to school with them.*)

126

I've always thought it telling that Robert and Margaret, who didn't grow up with us and moved South from outside, were the two voting for fairness. Robert asked me, *why didn't you vote for integration?* and I couldn't admit peer pressure. I had no better answer.

In my head I echoed the question, *Yeah, why not?*

****

The next year our class was integrated, by one girl, as we expected. Wilucia Green was, in fact, a prominent Black doctor's daughter, and rumor had it there was a lot of NAACP planning behind her school switch.

There was no big protest, no screaming mob, and from what I saw of the White kids' side, no big deal. But I heard much later from other White kids Wilucia got more than her share of being bumped on the staircase and in the hallways during class changes.

Turns out Wilucia's sister integrated the junior high school the same year. A brave family. Years later, when Wilucia heard my regrets about not seeking her out during high school, she was surprised and, in a soft Southern way, hinted I was a big shot, and why would I be interested in her? I had never considered myself in that light before. It was a revelation. There could have been a slight rebuke there, too, maybe I was only interested in her because she was Black, but I didn't think so.

David McCurry transferred in from another district our senior year, making two Black students in a school of about 1,400 kids. David was more outgoing and seemed to have an easier time of it. It might have helped he was male, but I think Wilucia paved the way.

****

The end-of-year, school-wide pep rally. The assembled horde of

127

young Athens High Trojans were going home or to work for the summer. (Rarely commenting on the displayed ignorance of calling themselves Trojans from Athens. More than willing to smirk at being called Trojans.)

A gym full of kids with nothing to do but work off hormones and jitters. Cheerleaders wound up the crowd, which didn't need any help. Athletic letter-winners were recognized. And we were ready for the finale. The cheerleaders would play off one side of the gym, seniors and freshmen, against the other, us juniors and sophomores. Who could yell the loudest?

GOOOOOOOH! from the seniors and freshmen. *TROOOOH-JAANNS!* from the sophomores and juniors. Louder and louder. The seniors always won. Seniors were the judges. When they heard the announcement they'd won, a new chant broke out from their side.

THE LAST WHITE CLASS!! THE LAST WHITE CLASS!! **THE LAST WHITE CLASS!!**

The chant filled the high school gymnasium. A pep rally amok, lifted out of itself by the very power of sound.

Willie

He appeared from nowhere, but Stan and I assumed we knew where he came from. There was only one likely place.

Rock Springs Homes.

The Black housing project in back of the White high school. The kid must have hopped the baseball fence and come a distance across the field and down to the tennis courts. Crossing a number of taboos along the way.

****

Stan and I had been playing for an hour a few days after the pep rally when we spied the Black kid. It was summer vacation in a steam-bath, and Stan and I were well-matched. A lot of sets went five-seven or seven-nine. This was long before tiebreakers. We wore ourselves out every time we played. I was thin and wiry. Stan was bigger and had to carry more weight around the court.

Stan called out to the newcomer, *Hey, you wanna play? Jimmy always lasts longer than I do. You can use my racket.*

Stan is a gentleman, through and through.

The kid said, *Sure.* He walked over to Stan's side of the court and Stan handed him his racket, as if Black boys and White boys played together all the time. *I'm Willie*, said the new boy.

Stan completed the introductions *I'm Stan and that's Jimmy over there.*

Nice to meet y'all, Willie said, and shook Stan's hand. *Nice to meet you too*, I added from the far side.

I was jealous of Stan. I'd never shaken hands with a Black kid. I'd never had the opportunity to do it, or to turn it down. Some White people would refuse to shake.

I said to Willie, *Let's hit it around some first.* He was cool about it. It's common in pick-up sports for there to be a noncompetitive start-up time while people sort each other out. Sometimes that's what we do, merely shoot around if it's b-ball, or throw it around if it's football, or hit it around if it's tennis.

Willie was athletic, you could see it. And he had to be brave, coming down to a White court like he did. And he was well-built, more to my body plan than Stan's, but sort of in between the two of us.

Stan and I went way back. He went to a different grammar school, but we'd gone to the same church since nursery school and played together in the neighborhood and at the Y. There was some imaginary line between his house and mine which sent kids one way or the other to grade school. But we got together a lot.

I had an OK backhand. Willie had none. He had to run around balls to his left and hit them forehanded because hitting balls from his weak side drove every one out-of-bounds somewhere. However, he was quick, so once he figured out the run-around, he could keep a ball in play.

After a while I hollered over, *Hey, you wanna hit some serves?*

Willie wasn't too sure about it. He took a beat or two to say yes, and I began to think tennis might actually be new to him. In which case, he was more than a merely good athlete. Serving is not an easy skill to master, but he was going to try.

I'd never seen anything like Willie's first attempt. He wrapped the racquet behind his head like it was a baseball bat, tossed the ball up like he might have done as a young kid practicing baseball alone, throwing himself pop flies or throwing himself hitting practice, but not as high. Willie took a soft swing at the ball. He hit it, but it went straight into the net. I hit him the spare ball I kept in my pocket. Willie caught it, went through the same motions but tried to hit the ball a little higher, and hit the ball out long.

You could see Willie trying to keep his cool but being ticked off at himself. We've all been there, trying to look good for strangers. It was probably worse with the unspoken Black/White stuff hanging in the air.

Willie tried a different approach, sort of an *If I'm going down, at least I'm going to go down swinging.* He tossed the ball up again, but this time didn't try to aim or hit softly. He took a homerun swing.

The ball flashed off the racket like a laser. Straight over the net. Straight into the box. And straight past me who could only gape and stare.

Ace! I yelled. *Man, what a great serve! Where were you keeping that?*

I was glad I had yelled *man* instead of *boy.* I didn't think about it when I did it; I got lucky. If I had yelled *boy,* the odds were good it would

130

have been misinterpreted. This was the only time in my life so far I'd ever been able to play with a Black kid. I was glad I didn't screw it up stupidly.

I thought Willie's serve was weird and wonderful. It was clear Willie had never had any lessons, so he was only doing what made sense. Hit it like you would a baseball. A sport he obviously knew. But who would think it would go in?

Serve again, Willie. I want another shot at that.

I don't know what Willie was thinking, but I would have been wondering what would happen this time. I would have thought I got lucky. But I would have had to try again, and hope.

Willie wound up in his batter's stance once again, threw the ball up and hit another ace. Or at least it should have been, but this time I was ready and hit it back. Willie, surprised, had to run to chase it down, but he too got it back over and in. This was fun. We actually kept the rally going longer than any of the times Stan and I did. Finally, the ball went out. We were both huffing and puffing.

Hey Willie, let's take a water break, I yelled over. I was worn out.

None of us saw what was coming next.

****

There were no White and colored drinking fountains at the courts. There were no water fountains whatsoever. You drank from a hose at the football practice field.

When we got to the hose-bib, Stan loosened the faucet to let the water run and cool the hot hose. Warm hose-tasting water is not a popular drink.

Willie, probably mindful he was in a no-man's land and White folks were peculiar about their drinking fountains, said, *I'll drink last.*

Stan and I replied as a chorus, *No, you go first.* I think we both liked Willie and wanted him to know we weren't total rednecks. (In my class-conscious stereotyping, I thought you wouldn't see a lot of vicious rednecks on tennis courts, but now I'm sure I was both wrong and blind.) Stan was also being his generous self.

Willie stuck to his guns. *No, it's OK. Y'all go on.*

We three were caught up in the moment, nobody catching the absurdity of fighting over pride of second place, drinking warm water from a dirty lawn hose. Who knew where the hose had been?

****

Nevertheless, there could have been a lot of cogitating going on around the hose. Willie could have been thinking, *Well, we could go White, Black, White, splitting the difference.* Then he might think, *but what if the first White boy makes fun of the other White boy later on, and spreads the story around?* Willie had no way of knowing how long Stan and I had been friends.

Stan was clearly thinking, *Man, we could do this After-You-Alphonse dance forever.*

I was thinking, *I don't know how Stan feels about this. We've been friends since we were tiny, but we've never talked about Blacks. What if he cares about not drinking behind Black people? He said for Willie to go first, but he could have done it out of manners.*

Finally, I said, *Willie, it's OK, but I'm going to go ahead and drink before we drain the school down.* And Stan followed me, and Willie drank last. It was awkward at first, but we soon relaxed. We had honored the social code, but we had also sort of respected each other.

****

Hey, y'all ever go bowling? Willie asked when he had his fill.

Yeah, sometimes, Stan answered. *In PE they take the whole class out to Beechwood Lanes and teach us how.*

132

I've never been bowling, Willie said.

Stan and I glanced at each other—both amazed. A guy our age who had never been bowling didn't make sense to us. We had bowled more than a few times before the school took us. There wasn't enough to do in Athens that you wouldn't try bowling. No light dawning for the White boys yet.

There isn't any place I can go, Willie said, like we were maybe a little obtuse.

Aftermath

The hot air sighed, hanging heavy and still. Then Stan and I caught on. There was the Harlem theater for Blacks, and they could also sit in the balcony of the Georgia, but there was no bowling alley for Black people. The closest a Black boy could get was pin-setting in the dive poolhall and bowling alley downtown, where White boys delighted in trying to hit the setters with the ball or the pins.

If it had been a White-White situation, the right course of action would have been clear. Invite Willie to come bowling with you. Was it different because Willie was Black? Was it different because the bowling alleys hadn't been integrated? Would it be dangerous? What did Kelley teach at the Y about the Samaritan and loving your neighbor, and what a neighbor was?

I said, *Let's go bowling. You got a phone?*

We exchanged phone numbers and by unspoken agreement everybody called it a day. Stan and I walked up the hill toward the school. Willie walked up the hill the other way toward the project. He might have figured he'd never hear from either of us again.

I had absolutely no idea what I was going to do.

Five long summer days later, I had it thought out, *kinda*. I would go to Beechwood Lanes and talk to the manager first before calling Willie, and I would definitely not just show up out there with Willie. If the manager said they weren't integrated and weren't planning to integrate, I would call Willie and tell him.

That part, the telling Willie, didn't feel quite right. My gut said to go ahead and try to integrate the place whether the bowling alley wanted it done or not. But I was honestly scared. Scared of making people mad.

On the other hand, I liked Willie and I didn't want to offend him either. It wasn't fair Stan and I could bowl at a couple of different places, and the school took us bowling, but Willie couldn't bowl anywhere.

What would happen once I talked to the manager wasn't clear. But going out to talk to him would be doing something. Stan and I hadn't talked about it any, and I assumed it was up to me if we were going to do anything or not. I had been the one to start down the do-something road. I had jumped into the silence and made the offer.

Next day I drove out to Beechwood. In the daytime the place was almost deserted. I walked up to the counter where you asked for a lane, and bowling shoes if you needed them. I wasn't sure how this conversation was going to go.

May I help you? the manager asked archly, thinking I was some new kind of day-bowling space-case teenager.

Yes sir, I burbled brightly. Never hurts to be polite. It's the Southern way. The grease of discourse. *Would it be alright if I brought a Black friend of mine to bowl sometime?*

Brilliant, I thought. I'm sure he was hoping I would ask if we could de-segregate his place. *Hey everybody come on down to Beechwood. We're integrating tonight! Bring your best robes!* My opening was weak and namby-pamby. Maybe I should have been telling the manager what I was

134

going to do and not asking permission. Maybe my ambivalence about the whole enterprise was showing.

I was surprised at the manager's response.

I wouldn't want you to, but the new law will say I'd have to let you in. I'd do that, but I'd put you down at the far end lane. This was 1964, right before the Civil Rights Act passed.

I had been somewhat prepared for yelling and screaming. I expected some kind of a *No* answer.

What I wasn't prepared for was a calm *Yes* which made some kind of sense to a White Southerner. The man had a business to run. He would do what the law said he had to do, but he'd keep the Black boy as far away as possible from the rest of his customers, many of whom wouldn't care what the brand-spanking-new federal law said and would object to a Black person being anywhere in the building, except behind the pin-setting machines or janitoring.

I almost stuttered as I said, *Thank you, sir, that would be fine with us.* The further away we were from other potentially angry bowlers the better. I didn't want to admit it, but I was a little disappointed in the man's calm acceptance of the new reality. Now I had to go through with the plan.

The drive home was a blur.

****

It took several more days to come to terms with my own new truth. I had either to admit I was a coward, morally and physically, or I had to call Willie. On the third day I called.

Hello, may I speak to Willie? Oh, when will he be home? OK. Could you ask him to call Jimmy at 2524 when he gets home? It's about bowling. Thank you ... Bye.

I can only imagine what happened or didn't happen in Willie's house.

Whether someone lost the message, or whether Willie had only wanted to see what would happen if he made it clear how sheltered we were, or whether his parents said *No! And don't call him back either!*

I didn't appreciate what his parents would have known instantly—how large a danger we were flirting with.

But when Willie never called back, I was relieved.

Bats, Balls, and a Banjo

Merle's mom was a warm, easy-going woman who saw no point in keeping up with every little move we made, and Merle's kid sister wasn't a pest. So, we practiced at his house. The '60s folk revival was square-dancing through the country, and Athens was allemandering right along. The seniors ahead of us were planning a hootenanny fundraiser.

Merle and I thought we might do a song or two. He had a lustrous old archtop Silvertone guitar which put out a lot of mellow sound. Everybody else had nylon-stringed folk guitars or electrics, so Merle's steel-string was different. I had a Sears and Roebuck five-string banjo which I loved, but which didn't love me.

I wasn't making much progress on it, or on keeping up with Merle. Taking a break from the music by shooting lethargic hoops in the side-yard shade, Merle suddenly started talking about the commotion downtown.

What we ought to do is take a bat and go down there and beat some sense in their heads.

I knew what he was talking about. Blacks were starting to march around the Palace Theater, the home of the Saturday morning Kiddie show, the theater which had no seating for Blacks, segregated or otherwise. Like Br'er Fox in the *Uncle Remus* tales, I just lay low. Merle didn't know about my encounter with Willie at the tennis courts.

136

They got a theater, why do they want to come to ours?

I didn't want to answer the rhetorical question. So I acted like people do when they don't want to answer; I feigned ignorance. *I don't know.*

I also didn't ask Merle why he thought we would necessarily win a street fight even if we had a bat each.

Merle kept at it... *I get so tired of this. First it was the university, next it was our school. Now it's the movies. I only want to get through school and have some fun.*

Yeah, I like having fun, too. But are we going to have fun at the hootenanny or embarrass ourselves to death?

I'm going to have fun, chickenshit. Now get your butt back into my room and encourage your worthless five-string to make something like music, if you can.

I still had doubts about my music-making abilities, but at least we got the chord changes together.

What Else I Might Remember

From the summer of '64.

Hitchhiking back from Mountain City, a dance-hall town in the mountains, to Big Y Camp with Stan. As Leaders of cabins of younger campers, we had small privileges. Occasional nights off being chief among them. Traffic was light on Highway 23 and we were tired of walking. The road was straight, we could see and hear for miles, not that there was much to hear except the crickets. So naturally we laid down on the center white stripe, feeling the heat of the asphalt, and watched stars shoot by.

We heard the thrum of a motor before we saw the lights, getting up slowly, and sticking out our thumbs as we edged towards the southbound shoulder. The car slowed and stopped. A woman on the passenger side looked us over, cryptically saying *You boys shouldn't be out tonight. Hop in.*

And we did. *Where you headed?* asked the guy driving. They seemed like an older married couple. Probably no threat to us. Stan said *Down to the Y camp road, but anywhere along the way would be fine.* Mountain City was only fifteen miles from camp. We could walk the whole way if we had to. The lady said *We're gonna turn off at T'rora Circle. Run you right by there.* Stan and I sang in chorus, *Wonderful! Thank you.*

We rode on in silence for a while, but soon one of us in the back asked the question on our minds.

Why shouldn't we have been out tonight? We were just taking some time off up at Mountain City. The driver sneaked a peek at his wife and gave a barely perceptible nod. She looked over her shoulder at both of us and said merely four words, *There's trouble out tonight.* We understood her comment was the end of the conversation.

Soon enough we came to Terrora Circle and the entrance to the Y Camp road. We exited the car and said our thank-yous, nice-meeting-yous, and good-byes. When we were done and the car had pulled away, we wondered to each other *What trouble?* And pondered it back to our cabins. The date was July 11, 1964, the day before my seventeenth birthday. A few days later, Stan and I heard the trouble was 70 miles away, back towards Athens, but we had no idea how the couple up in the mountains knew it was going to happen.

****

Other things I might remember. White rumors of Black carhops at the new *Varsity* drive-in spitting in your food when they brought it to your car.

The rebirth of a local Klan. Klansmen carrying-on with their pistols and walking alongside Black protesters at the segregated *Varsity* hotdog

138

palaces. Blacks able to work as carhops, but not able to be served where they worked. Klan members shot-gunning Black housing projects and night-riding in KKK-emblazoned rigs.

It didn't register with me until they murdered somebody.

Lieutenant Colonel Lemuel Penn of the National Reserves.

Returning home to D.C. from training at Fort Benning near Columbus in South Georgia. Lt. Col. Penn had spent the entire two-week training on-base—hoping to avoid racial trouble in town. Following the cautious path, Penn, Charles E. Brown, and John D. Howard decided to make the drive north a straight-through run. And to get off US 29. Too many small towns.

They were unlucky. A bigger town became the problem.

In Athens, their out-of-town D.C. plates and Black skins attracted the attention of the night-riders, a self-appointed security team of the local cell, Klavern 244. The Klansmen made the Reservists out to be some of Lyndon's boys come to assert their new freedoms under the Civil Rights Act.

The Klansmen watched as the Black men switched drivers in the middle of downtown, by the Confederate War Dead memorial. When the D.C. plates started moving again, the insecurity squad followed, keeping their distance, and keeping track because Martin Luther King Jr. might be trying to make Georgia a testing ground for the new civil rights law.

Twenty-four miles outside Athens, where Highway 172 crossed the Broad River, the Klansmen pulled alongside the Black men and let loose with two shotguns, killing Penn instantly but miraculously missing Brown and Howard.

White middle-class Athens treated it as a low-class Madison County problem. The killers deliberately waited until they were past the Athens/Clarke County line to throw the scent off.

It didn't matter. The FBI found the Athens Klavern, their hangouts, and the weak link. The driver of the Klan car. Finding him didn't matter either. The trial judge unconstitutionally allowed the two shooters to testify without cross examination; a key witness wouldn't testify; and the driver recanted his confession. The all-White, all-male Madison County jury didn't convict.

White people in both counties ranted in a fury when the murder got retrospective ink on the fiftieth anniversary. For the ones who commented online, it was more about anything but the murder. The county feud. Raking up the past. Irrelevant to anything in today's world. Blaming Madison County, when the criminals were from Athens/Clarke County. Discrimination against any White male age eighteen to sixty-five.

Few columnists checked in with the local Black communities.

It took a while, but the two gunmen finally served about six years in Federal penitentiaries for violating Penn's civil rights. The driver never stood trial.

The date of the shooting? July 11, 1964.

What I Do Remember

From the summer of '64? An invitation and a trip to the lake.

Out of the blue, Millie—the peppy newcomer I'd been flirting with in Physics—popped out with, *Would you like to go water-skiing next Saturday, the day after school's out?*

I was startled. Startled because I didn't think we were so far along. Startled further because she took the initiative. Delighted because it saved me a lot of fretting about whether I wanted to move the relationship along, and if I did, when and how?

It would be up at Lake Lanier with me, Ann, and Steve. Ann and her folks have the boat.

Steve was one of my best friends from cowboy days. Suddenly I did want to move our bond along, and she was doing it for me. And *water-skiing!* I loved being pulled behind a boat. I got up the first time somebody showed me how and was enraptured. Having no access to a motorboat myself, I was dependent on the kindness of strangers for any fossil-fueled watersports.

This would be my dream date.

****

Ann's dad and mom were willing to drive us up and drive the boat for us (and disappear while Ann, Steve, Millie, and I picnicked and swam after skiing).

I said yes without thinking about asking Mom. I could tell her later.

That Saturday was gorgeous. It wasn't yet technically summer. Early June in the South is a sensual time with trees and flowers blooming in soft or showy colors; a subtle blend of moisture, plant sex, humus, and renewal delighting the nose.

The drive up to Lake Lanier was easy in the mid-'60s. Everything wasn't a sub-suburb of Atlanta, and I loved riding through the country. I always had, since the days with Dad. Somewhere along the way, Millie's hand found its way into mine, and it felt nice. Well actually more than nice.

It seemed somehow preludish.

****

We traveled out of my home range — the area explored on sailing trips and Scout adventures. I was surprised and delighted to see Lake Lanier had causeways and bridges. I never knew. Families parked old sedans and pickups well off the road and fished and picnicked at the grassy shoreline, an easy walk downslope from their rigs. A later, different vision of Seurat's *A Sunday on La Grande Jatte.*

The skiing was a blast. Ann was adept with two skis or one, and her dad was at home gently handling the boat for the inexperienced rest of us. Millie was hopeless, never managing to stay up for more than a second, but a good sport about it, and Steve and I both enjoyed zipping along behind the boat and staying upright until we got too rambunctious about crossing the wake.

We were sun-basted, waterlogged, and tired by the time we quit. But we would probably be out there still if Ann's dad hadn't reminded us lunchtime had long passed and there was a good picnic waiting for us at the launch ramp. The last skier climbed in and we headed back to the ramp.

****

That day gently rolled on. Reminiscent of the picnickers at the causeway, we ate our picnic on a gentle slope between the boat ramp and a mellow cove. Ignoring the one-hour rule, we swam as soon as the food was gone.

Tired and replete, we lumbered out of the water for more sun-bathing on the shore, enjoying the unmerciful teasing Steve had to endure as two pre-teen girls tormented him about the hair on his back. And, too early, it was time to go. If we didn't leave soon it would be dark when we got home.

The route back was geographically the reverse of the route up, but it had a different impact. The day wasn't done.

We passed through miniscule Dawsonville, the post-office town for the boat club, crossed the Boling Bridge, and reached the causeway. And it was like seeing a reel out of order in a movie.

Life changed, and we saw the dark ending.

The cars on the causeway were at bad angles off the road. The family picnicking and fishing on the grassy shore wasn't in sight. But their white and red checked blanket was, wadded up and tire-treaded. Run-over by a car.

A car. Unbelievably far off the road.

Over there. Upside down in the shallow water. Wheels no longer spinning. The car that hit the blanket. *Did it hit the family?*

Oh God, Yes. There's a body by the blanket.

Yards, yards away from the highway. The straight and unobstructed highway, with perfect visibility. How in the world; why in the world would a car leave the highway and find the one family left on a gentle bucolic slope?

We pulled way, way over and Ann's dad got out. We couldn't help ourselves. We got out, too. Another car was pulled over ahead of us. Ann's dad went to talk with the one person left standing. Turned out to be the driver of the parked car, not of the car wheels-up in the water. He clearly wasn't a family member.

I was a Scout. I was supposed to know what to do here. I knew I was turning white, and I could feel the blood leaving my head and a lightheaded queasiness replacing it. And while I retained a vague idea of what needed doing, I couldn't do it. None of us kids said a word. Simply got back in the car and silently, secretly hoped Ann's dad was finding everything had been done.

He came back to the car, and he, too, didn't say anything. He just started the car and, noticeably slowly, and abundantly carefully, drove back onto the road. I've always wanted to believe our hopes had come to life—that someone had gone for the police and an ambulance; and that the grown-ups did what should have been done. But I've never rested easy about it.

***

143

No one broke the silence for a long time, and when they did, they spoke of anything but the accident.

I had made it through Dad's death and Mom's folding. But this. This seemed gratuitously cruel, even for a random universe. A family enjoying life as we think it should be enjoyed, wiped out by a car which shouldn't have been anywhere near them. I didn't want to think about it, and didn't, but I was shaken, rattled, and rolled—and my gut added, *Told you so*.

****

Could be the end of the story, but life can be stranger yet.

The light was fading by the time we reached Jefferson, thirty miles from Athens. The road home seemed slower. Everybody was subdued, and Millie's hand found its way back into mine. As the headlights came on, Millie turned as if to whisper to me but, instead, her mouth found my neck.

She was kissing me. Finding my lips, too. This lasted a long time. It was wonderful. It was so wonderful I only halfway thought about how strange it was to be doing this as if we were the only ones in the car. As if there were no unfamiliar grown-ups in the front seat chauffeuring us around. As if Ann and Steve weren't right next to us. As if we weren't in shock from a horrifying accident.

This must be what Mom called *forward behavior*. It might even be the start of the fabled primrose path. Then Millie moved her soft hand inside my shirt. What a lovely path.

I don't think she and I stopped until the car pulled into the driveway at my house. I certainly don't remember stopping. But I know we did somehow. Our front porch light was on and the door was swinging open as I started disentangling to get out. Caroline was practically skipping down the walk to greet me.

She was home from the university for a weekend, which was special.

144

Her face shone with delight and expectation, and, despite the dim porch-light, you could see the shine turn crimson, as she blushed furiously. Something in my body posture and Millie's gaze told Caroline that Millie and I hadn't quite been done saying goodnight.

I loved Caroline for the blush and stammered apology. Somehow it confirmed something important had happened.

It had, but I couldn't rid myself of a qualmy unease attached to the bloodied family hanging over my sensual pleasure.

God has a very strange sense of humor.

9. Idyll on the River

The River

The university overshadowed everything else in the town, so it was hard for outsiders to recognize Athens as a river town, but it was. The Oconee River flows around Athens, but, when I lived there, the town ignored the river except when it invaded the land beyond its banks, or when we needed to dump our sewage.

The river, deservedly or not, had a reputation as a moving cesspool and we were not encouraged to play in it.

Didn't stop us.

Kelley took us canoeing and snake-catching every summer at Pine Tops. The river curved around one long edge of the camp. He never cautioned us about the Oconee's nastiness. Giving warning was our parents' job and they probably overdid it. Bubbie and I made a memorable bike run out to a stretch we thought would be safe. Played in the water. Ate our sack lunches and rode the railroad ties and ballast back home. The ride home on an active rail line was much scarier than getting a mouthful of Oconee River water.

And despite the town ignoring it when I lived there, the river was a presence in its history.

Athens was located in our special piece of Georgia Piedmont because the Oconee provided water, power, fertile land, and shoals for fording. Through the pre-war period, the war I grew up calling the War-Between-the-States, and Reconstruction, it powered mills and factories. But by the time I came along, its economic importance had disappeared.

The factories and mills no longer depended on it for power. And it flooded, smelled rotten, never ran clear, and chose disturbing colors to display instead. I found it hard to close my eyes and nose to it.

That said, I never understood the river when I lived there. I didn't need to. I thought since the Oconee was on the east of town when we went to Winterville (where our wealthy chicken-farmer friends lived) and on the west when we went to Atlanta or Pine Tops, and it was also on the north when we went to the junkyard, and on the south when we went to Watkinsville, that it surrounded the town.

I never worried about the hydrodynamics of a river which could run in a complete circle. I did, however, absorb a vague uneasiness about its power and nastiness.

I remember ruinous floods and the ugly, opaquely dark Nehi orange-drink color that was plain wrong. I could have understood red—Georgia being famous for both its red clay hills and their erosion—but orange was so off it reinforced a sense of corrosive contamination emanating from the bottom land. (I knew there was orange clay—my white socks were stained orange from the university's clay tennis courts. But it didn't belong in the river. There it was ugly.)

And yet, despite my foreboding perceptions of the river, I could not resist its pull. Call it a willing suspension of belief. *If I go upstream or downstream a little bit, I'll be fine.*

Turns out there are actually three rivers around Athens, each called The Oconee. So, I have some justification for my confusion. The North Oconee rises in the mountains up halfway between Maysville and Constantine, flows southeast toward Athens, makes a gentle arc from north of Athens around to the east and back to the south where it joins the Middle Oconee, which has come in from the northwest and defined Athens on the west. The confluence of the North Oconee and the Middle Oconee south of town marks the beginning of the Oconee River proper.

An aerial sketch would show the town happily sitting in the fork of a left-leaning Y formed by the Oconee river system, which, despite what I've learned as an adult, will always be the singular Oconee to me.

In effect, the river cradled the town, almost as the town cradled me. The town tried to protect me, and when it couldn't, it tried its best to heal me. Unlike the river which could be destructive, there was no harm to me in the town.

In my memories, Athens is always sunny and warm and the people always pleasant, mannered, caring, and thoughtful. When the troubles struck my family, the town pulled together to get us by, and for years I assumed it did the same for others. I now understand boys on the other sides of color and class lines wouldn't necessarily see the town bathed in light the way I do, but for me it always came through.

Beginnings of a Raft

The raft started out simpler than the river. There were only three differences between Huck Finn's raft and our Explorer Post's raft. One, Huck's raft floated. Two, his raft was three times as big as ours, and finally, nobody threw the poles overboard from Huck's raft.

But it was a grand adventure. In fact, the first adventure of newly registered Athens, GA, Explorer Post Number One.

Explorer Scouts were, at the time, the Boy Scout branch for older boys. (Now the branch is called *Venturing*.) A group of us who aged out of Boy Scouts wanted to continue doing outdoorsy things together, so we cajoled the First Methodist Church into sponsoring an Explorer Post and helping us find an adult leader. They did it nicely.

We'd done canoeing and water-skiing, but we hadn't done rafting. The type beginning like an old rabbit stew recipe, *First catch a rabbit*. For us, it was *First cut some trees*. We planned to follow-up with *When the logs have dried tie them together with genuine Boy Scout knots.* The white-water rubber rafting which evolved later had no place in our consciousness.

Given our small-town, hill country, river-rippled Southern roots, and despite the Oconee's spotty reputation, we decided to float our own orange river on this home-made timber raft. We figured it would take a year to cut the trees, trim them, cut them to length, let them dry (green trees don't float well), and make the trip. We thought there was a margin of error built into the schedule, barring disaster. We'd go from late spring to late spring. This was Georgia where spring was exceptionally nice, but late spring was the hot side of warm.

My friend Bruce's dad owned some river ground toward Watkinsville with some trees in need of thinning and which had a dirt road already bladed. We put our map-reading merit badges to use and calculated. If we put in where we would build the raft, we could float down the river and pull out where Highway 15 crossed the river. It would be a ten- or eleven-mile down-river run with a few riffles and a lot of bends, but we ought to be able to do it in a day.

We set a date for a weekend of log-cutting and started gathering tools.

No chainsaws allowed.

****

Our adult leader, John Bell—who had my heart immediately because he raced jalopies at the local dirt track—found an old bus and drove the whole post and our potpourri of implements of destruction out to Bruce's dad's land. We had axes, hatchets, machetes, brush hooks, two-man cross-cut saws, bow saws, loppers, pruners, and, of course, knives. Scouts and Explorers love knives.

I was familiar with these tools, but the difference between two of them was not obvious to everybody. An axe and a brush hook aren't

150

intended for the same tasks, though they're both edged implements for working outside. The brush hook is for clearing and grubbing shrubs and vines and small saplings. The axe's uses are well-known.

The brush hook blade is much thinner and lighter than the axe head and is attached parallel to the shaft, rather than crosswise. As you might guess, the blade has a hook to it, and the hook can be single-edged or edged on both inner and outer sides of the hook. The brush hook is not good for cutting trees or chopping.

The morning went well. We hacked our way through the underbrush to a couple of decent-sized trees, not too little to be useless, not too big to be beyond our felling abilities and equipment. By lunch break we had one down. After lunch we hauled the downed tree closer to the water and three of us stayed with the tree to start shaping it up for the raft, while the rest of the Post went back into the brush to work on another tree.

One of the twins in the Post and I were working the cross-cut saw on the butt end while another Explorer was lopping the branches off the trunk. He started down at the skinny end and worked his way toward us with the lopper. Somewhere along the way he changed tools. He got so close to me I started getting a little nervous. His swing was erratic, but having never had a great sense of self-preservation, I didn't say anything.

When I caught on, he was swinging with a brush hook, what little sense of my own mortality I had kicked in, but it was too late. He swung hard and the light-bladed brush hook didn't bite the tree but glanced off, still carrying a fair amount of energy. Enough energy to bite me hard.

Blood at the River's Edge

Bruce told me later it scared the bejabbers out of him. If I'd looked up a tad more it would have sliced my throat. As it was, it made an ugly impact right above my lip. Blood everywhere. The kid with the brush hook went white as a sheet.

Me too. Scouts went running and shouting. John Bell got the bus as close as he could, which was closer than most guys could have, while four Scouts were carrying me to him while Bruce pushed a dirty hanky against the rip in my face, trying to slow the blood. It was a long way to the hospital.

I don't remember the rest, till I got home. Definitely scared the be-jabbers out of Mom. I think no one called her, which I believed was always the right way to approach her—you didn't want her to have extra time to get wound up. I was starting to recover, but as soon as she saw me, she went white. Same as the brush hook wielder and I had when it happened. John Bell told her the docs said I'd be fine. They'd sewed me up, given me a tetanus shot, and said *when he starts shaving, the scar won't show.*

I'm not sure the last part was reassuring to her. It wasn't to me either because I was showing no signs of having to shave ever. (Besides which they were wrong. It remains visible.)

What buzzed her off, though, was the careless Explorer's mother not calling saying *I'm sorry, et cetera, et cetera.* I kept my mouth shut. The idea he would voluntarily tell his mom what had happened was crazy, and I didn't think anyone else was going to tell her either. So, he was off the hook, as far as his parents were concerned, and his mom should have been off the hook as far as other parents were concerned.

At home I got awkward and awe-struck visits from two girls. Mom didn't quite know what to make of them. She hinted their coming was improper, but how she got there I don't know. More likely, it was her not wanting girls hanging around me. Too much competition.

The Scouts went back there the next day and knocked another tree down and limbed it. (My little misadventure was nowhere near what constituted a show-slowing disaster.) I hated to miss the day of outdoor activity, but the truth was I was hurting, and, never to be admitted, shaken.

At school the next week, people wanted to hear the story. A tale of the blood-spattered brush hook, Bruce's gore-soaked rag, and the Explorers' four-man carry would have been cool. But I wasn't into it. I certainly didn't want to let on how scared I was, how much I couldn't remember, and how dumb I was to stay there within range of a brush hook in careless hands.

And yet, by the end of the week I was anxious to get back out there.

The Float

We had the logs cut and the raft assembled by the end of spring. And for the heck of it, we plopped it in the water. It was a heavy sucker, and the plopping involved a lot of pushing and shoving and slipping and sliding on a muddy bank, and no lifting after the first attempt.

The raft immediately sank like the *Lusitania*. Not without a trace, but it definitely sank. Wood doesn't always float. And our assemblage clearly needed more drying time.

Maybe something more than drying. We managed to get it up from the water and onto the bank, and with a clever thought, ropes, and extra oomph, up above the high-water mark. We did not want it to acquire more moisture. And there we left it, where it would—we hoped—dry out thoroughly while we went on with our high school lives until next spring.

Fortunately for us, Mr. Turkett, Bruce's dad, was a practical man and knew something about how the world worked. While we were trusting in the doubtful drying powers of a humid, shady riverside mudflat through a summer (good), fall (not as good), and winter/early spring (not good period), Mr. Turkett was making a contingency plan for us.

The fall was wet, as feared, and one weekend he gathered Bruce and a couple of other Explorers and made a run out to the raft. In the back of the pickup were some empty fifty-gallon drums. The old steel kind. When they came back, the drums were gone, and the raft floated. It didn't float high, but it floated.

Spring came. And it was time to actually make our run. To say we were excited is to understate matters. At least some of us. Others had either more sense or higher priorities or both. The crew who actually wanted to jump on a questionable raft and make an eight-hour run down a polluted river was noticeably smaller than the crew which built it.

As in sausage and law, something about being too close to the raft being made may have been in play.

The nine of us making the run had our lunches, our drinks (truly, no alcohol was involved or thought of with this straight-arrow group), and an omnipresent but unrecognized belief we were invincible.

That last part, the *invincible* part, was immediately challenged. As soon as we got the raft unstuck from the mud bar and into the water, and despite the 50-gallon drums underneath, we appeared Jesus-like, walking—or at least gliding—on the water. No sign of the raft. We were standing on the water and we were moving. Our ankles were wet. We knew there was a raft there somewhere, we could feel it beneath our soggy sneakers, but we couldn't always see it. It didn't want to float above the water, but sort of in it. Oh well, we were off.

Did you notice anything missing from my inventory of what we brought on the trip? Did we have life vests? No. Paddles? No. Cell phones? Didn't exist. Poles? A few after-thought sticks. Dry bags? Never heard of them. *Be Prepared*, the Scout Motto? Ignored. But we *were* off.

After a bit we calmed down; however, the first couple of river-bends and river-rocks got our adrenaline pumped right back up. The sticks were barely adequate for poling—we snapped two of them right away—and less than adequate for steering. And the river wasn't big or much interested in moving us along.

For the first part of the trip every time there was a curve or a rock there was an accompanying flurry of Scout activity as we tried to do something to make sure we got around the bend or avoided nailing the rock. The bends were easier. We smacked more than one rock.

And no doubt it would have been helpful if we agreed on what needed to be done. A disturbed ant hill shows the same kind of frenzy, but with more coordination.

Since we were running low on sticks, and surprisingly nobody had brought a hatchet, we developed a method to help us around bends without using our pole-substitutes. The Hendrix twins, math and physics geniuses both, suggested it. We crowded onto the back corner on the side we wanted to turn toward and sank that corner deeper. In fact, we could almost pop the diagonal corner completely out of the water. The increased drag of the sunken corner with us crowded on it helped the raft turn around the bend, and besides it gave us something to do.

And so we floated along...and along.

That river was going pretty slow, and we weren't going any faster than the water. In fact, what with the occasional rock encounter and what passed for maneuvering, we were going slower than the river.

And the snakes Bruce spotted weren't enough to keep us alert, or happy, or scared. We were drifting down the river, as we had planned, but a lot, lot slower than imagined. And with a lot more standing, since nobody wanted to just sit in the river, which is what sitting on the raft would turn out to be.

We started in the morning and had lunch somewhat past the sun's zenith. Later, though the light lingered like it does in the South, we could tell it was getting on toward dinner time, since we were more ravenous than usual. We'd left our watches behind, since none of us had one advertising *Good to 300 m.* Most of ours tended, instead, to fog over in a mere sprinkling.

Accordingly, while we knew how far we had to go in total, we had no idea how fast we were going, no idea how far we had gone, no river map, no idea how far we had yet to go, and no idea where we were, except of course we were on the Oconee, and somewhere ahead of us was the Highway 15 bridge. Where we would get out.

But darkness had crept in. Not full dark *dark*, but dark. We were running late. We could see each other, but of course not much of the raft since we hadn't seen much of the raft since we set off in bright daylight. We could see the river around us, but the riverbanks not so much.

Rocks would surprise us now, and when we got hung up on one of those, Roger, of the Hendrix twins, lost his glasses in the inevitable hysteria of action. The loss saddened at least half of us — the ones who had lost or crushed our glasses before. We tried to find Roger's, searching the sunken raft with our hands as the water flowed through us, but we suspected it would be a lost cause. It was.

Roger revived following a short period grieving and we continued our slow pace down the indolent river. Nightfall speeded the pace up, but only in heartrates and imagination. It made rocks, bends, and trees more interesting. They look different when you can't see them.

We never thought about how we would stop the raft when we reached the bridge. But by the time we saw its dim outline ahead we were seasoned rafters. We went to the back river-right corner of the raft and bent the raft's path toward the shallow water upstream of the bridge abutment. The raft beached like we knew what we were doing.

Tired, hungry, and satisfied, we hailed John Bell and Mr. Turkett, and the faithful old yellow bus, and bailed out.

10. Commencing

Downhill

If you walked from our house directly towards downtown, you'd see Cloverhurst went metaphorically downhill as you went literally down the hill. There were bigger, more ornate homes uphill from us and houses smaller and more modest than ours downhill. If you walked down to where Cloverhurst ended at Baxter Street you'd be in a Black neighborhood with unpainted, tin-roofed houses on short piles of rock or block, quarters like the ones in the hardscrabble country nearby.

It was years before I questioned whether the people in those houses were renters, or owners, and whether those paint-shy, rusted-roof dwellings might reflect on owners rather than the people who lived in them.

And more years before I thought through my value-laden assumptions about the worth of paint, shingles, and perimeter foundations.

But in my teens, without thinking about much, I often walked toward the bottom end of the street to get downtown or to the pool. Only once did I get jolted out of my mindless state. As I reached the near edge of the Black section, I glanced through the screen door of the first cabin and saw, to my wonder, a White classmate of mine. I could tell she wasn't visiting—there was no one else around. She lived there.

The girl looked up as my glance was leaving, and we were probably both painfully embarrassed. I was.

She had on a thin cotton shift—not stylish and not what she wore to school, and the dress and her cabin made me think she was poor, dirt poor. And her expression made me think she knew the judgements I was making. The first I understood there might be White people in town who were poorer than we were in our worst times.

And I wondered, in the terms of my White culture, what life was like for a White girl living on the edge of a colored shantytown. Did she and her family have the same community support we had?

College Choices

I was lucky to have choices. Caroline had the grades and the board scores to leave home, but her chosen school, Emory in Atlanta, said her financial need was so great they didn't have enough money to give her.

In my case, Mom kept saying *If it were up to me, you'd be going to Georgia*. Which I took to have two meanings: There wasn't enough family money for me to go anyplace else. And Mom wanted me to stay home.

But I had choices. Great SAT scores meant I was being recruited by a lot of schools including Davidson, a small liberal-arts, males-only, basketball-crazy college in North Carolina, and Michigan State, Dad's alma mater, which had a special program for National Merit semi-finalists. I had decided on Davidson when the Harrold family, of the doorstep vegetables and Homecoming clothes, suggested an alternative.

Tom, their youngest son and the one whose clothes fit me the best, was an upcoming senior at Columbia. He so loved the school and the New York experience he was on a personal mission to make sure more Georgia kids got a shot at it. He approached me and Stan. I bit. Stan didn't.

With a little scrambling I was able to get the application in on time, and I was accepted.

With a full ride.

That was the key. No money from the family required. No loans to pay back. I had to work, but I was used to work. Transportation would be an issue, but I was sure I could handle it. Tom would take me the first year. And I would live in the cheapest dorm-room on campus, eating in the cafeteria where I would work. Had to beat Mom's cooking.

Columbia had a *needs-blind* admissions policy making my enrollment possible, in great contrast to Caroline's experience at Emory. The recruiting call from the swimming coach surprised me more than the acceptance. The full ride shouldn't have surprised me, but it did. I hadn't fully understood what a *needs-blind* policy could mean.

I loved the prestige involved in being accepted into an Ivy League school, but I was leery about spreading the word around. It would not go over well in Athens. Harvard or Princeton maybe, but not New York City. The nastiest soul of Yankee-dom. Too fast-talking, too pushy, too mercenary, too Jewish. And from Mom especially, *so far!*

If You're Making a Change

Make as big a change as possible. My stock answer to the *Why?* questions. *Why would you leave the South? Why would you go to a city? Why would you leave your mom?* I could have made Davidson work financially, but it would not have had enough cultural difference and physical distance from home for what I thought I needed. Because nobody knew how much I needed to get out (since I wasn't letting on), I got a lot of questions about my choice.

At the time, I thought my answer made sense, and also reduced follow-up questions. Making sense to me still didn't make the answer a popular choice.

And I had no idea of the psychic toll I was in for. If I let myself think—as I was raised to think—that I was abandoning Mom and Mary Win, I would become paralyzed. Instead, I floated along with the acceptable rationale I was merely a bright, economically disadvantaged

159

Southern boy taking advantage of a rare opportunity. The conflict would catch me later.

So, Mary Win Can Vote?

In the spring of '65, while my little insular high school world was focused on college admissions, finding summer work, finding a job, or what to do about the draft, a lot of the adult realm across the US and the world was watching Selma, Alabama, only 275 miles away.

The fire-hosings, clubbings, teargassings, dog-siccings, and killings in reaction to the marches there generated a rogue wave of public support for enforceable voting rights protection. Rogue in size and strength to everyone. Rogue in surprise only to clueless White Southerners and their supporters. Although absorbed in my personal dramas, I was aghast at the intensity of hatred directed at people who only wanted to vote.

Of course, the Whites who said it was about more than voting were right. It was always about more than riding in busses, eating at lunch-counters, or voting.

It was, as the Whites who fought so ferociously against it understood, about destroying a way of life.

But what's wrong with destroying a way of life based on dehumanizing other people? A point of view I owe to my friend Margaret, who voted for integration back in tenth grade.

As a Voting Rights Act of 1965 became a more likely possibility, Aunt Ellen from across the street came visiting and I caught enough of her conversation with Mom to question it.

Win, have you thought about registering Mary Win to vote? I was astounded and perplexed. *They're going to try and register more coloreds to vote...* and she trailed off.

I started putting it together. With the Voting Rights Act in view—to the White South's chagrin—Aunt Ellen, despite her sweet White soul, was going to be part of a rear-guard action to do what she could to minimize its impact.

She wanted Mary Win to vote, as part of a presumed White bloc. Her job as a county social worker put her in touch with many White families like ours with children of physical but not mental age. She was going to try and put her network to use.

The thought Mary Win should be allowed—no, encouraged—to vote seemed so wrong, it took me a minute to fully catch up, but I did. Black voter registration drives were gearing up in anticipation of the Act. From a Southern White mindset, Aunt Ellen's response made perfect sense: if *They* were going to be registering people who weren't qualified to vote—Blacks, because they were Black, couldn't possibly be qualified—then *We* should do the same (register the White mentally handicapped, who would presumably vote as *We*—right-thinking White folk—told them to).

Today, I won't defend my assumption at the time that developmentally disabled people shouldn't be encouraged to vote. But in 1965, it was undeniably what I believed about Mary Win. It would have been like giving Mom two votes.

Which I'm sure was the point.

Star Teacher

Graduation week finally came, and my former French II teacher and current student body advisor, Madame Cole, gave me a copy of Fowler's *Modern English Usage* as a surprise graduation gift. The inscription was in French and read (my translation):

Les meilleurs voeux toujours à mon "Étoile" favorite—un vrai savant...Best wishes always to my favorite "Star"—a true scholar, a young

161

Christian gentleman, and a great person in every sense. May you always keep your good qualities! May you continue full of courage in the struggle to the truth and the highest knowledge!

I did not expect the gift, much less such an admiring and flowery tribute from Madame Cole. Neither did I expect her insightful choice of gifts, nor, especially, the subtle humor in both the choice and the inscription.

She was not known for her humor, but for her dedication. She and I knew I had not done well in her French II class. In fact, I earned two Cs. I had never gotten a C in an academic subject before.

Since Madame Cole was student body advisor and I was student body president, we worked together closely, and she knew me well. I knew she had wanted me to go on to French III, but she understood my choice not to.

Her gift of Fowler's compendium was a neat reference both to my love of wordplay in English and a graceful but tongue-in-cheek bow to my preference for English over her French. The inscription was also, I think, pointedly a bit beyond my French skills.

Those Cs, by the way, were well deserved. I put more time and energy into talking with Millie beside me than I did into conjugating verbs.

Madame Cole grasped the situation. She separated me from Millie and put me in the back row with a good and sober student. Who did not prove immune to my new-found garrulousness. But a new, valedictorian-level transfer student seated next to us did. My fun decreased, but my grade climbed to a B.

****

Eccentric though it may seem, I greatly appreciated Madame Cole's efforts to rein me in. I could have done better in French and she knew it. And I could have comported myself better in her class, and she knew that, too. While I never told her of my appreciation, she might have understood.

You see, there's another subtle piece of humor in her inscription. She says *Best wishes to my favorite Star* (Étoile). The capital is significant. I had won designation as the school's STAR student. The kid with the highest Scholastic Aptitude Test score.

And I had selected her as my STAR teacher, the one who meant the most to my academic development. These were state awards and included a reception in Atlanta with the other STAR pairs, and congratulations from people like the governor. Also included was a bus trip around the state with the other pairs.

I was on fire the day I took those SAT College Board tests and couldn't wait to get my scores. The tests had seemed reasonable and fun. I was delighted when my scores were good enough to win the STAR award.

However, it left me with a dilemma.

****

I had had outstanding teachers at Athens High.

Mrs. Harden, who made Algebra I make sense; Mrs. Moore, who made Advanced Algebra, and Probability and Statistics, interesting; Mrs. Pickett, who opened our eyes to Drama, a personal style of writing, and a lifetime of pleasure with words and words in action; Mr. Carter, who nurtured an interest in how things work and why, and permitted Millie's and my shameless flirting in his Physics class; Mrs. Maxwell, who made History more than dates, battles, and treaties, and who had the courage to bring up forbidden topics.

And Mrs. Cole, who made it about doing your best.

Mrs. Maxwell was going to get a two-page spread in the 1964 yearbook, and it would be well-deserved. She had been a STAR teacher at

163

least twice before and was a truly gifted educator. Who else could have gotten us to open up on integration and segregation as well as she did?

But I chose Madame Cole, because in my entire school history from Barrow Elementary through my last year of high school, and within my family, no one (outside of Kelley) had called me on my shit (and he would not have approved of my language).

I was coasting, and I had been doing so for several years, dodging the reputedly hard courses, and studying a bit for the tests in everything else. Learning and public schooling came easy to me, too easy it turned out when I jumped to Columbia, but Columbia was still in the future.

Madame Cole was my STAR teacher because she saw through me and liked me anyway, but she wanted me to learn something from her about working and studying and mastering.

Although I refused her challenge, I understood it, and respected her for issuing it. I missed her kind of understanding in my life and choosing her for the STAR role prepared me to make a good decision about Bertie, a young woman in my future who would also call me on my shit, and would agree to become my wife, despite it.

Madame Cole and I went to Atlanta and enjoyed the reception, but (and I should have seen it coming), she didn't come on the bus trip. She didn't want to leave her students for so long.

Nietzsche on the Bus

Virginia, one of the girls on the STAR bus trip, was different. Most of us, girls and boys, were high-achievers but trying hard not to be overt nerds. Virginia didn't mind being considered different. She kept herself slightly apart from the rest of us, reading from *The Portable Nietzsche*. She also dressed simply with casual elegance, contrasting noticeably with the collegiate style we sheep primped so hard for. I sat with her for a couple of days and got more surprises.

The Nietzsche might have been for show, but she seemed serious about it. She quoted to me and showed me underlined passages, reading to me and asking what I thought.

But what made me sit up and take notice was her troubles with her family. She was writing pro-civil rights letters to the *Albany Herald* (arch-defender of segregation) and joining demonstrations. According to what I thought I knew, the struggle in Albany was over. Dr. King had left town in August 1962, and hadn't been back.

But the locals were still at it. The Student Nonviolent Coordinating Committee (SNCC) field secretary Charles Sherrod made it plain, *Now I can't help how Dr. King might have felt, ... but as far as we were concerned, things moved on. We didn't skip one beat.* In fact, Black voter registration efforts were so successful that—two months following King's departure—African American businessman Thomas Chatmon secured enough votes in the election for a city commission seat to force a run-off election. The following spring the city commission removed all segregation statutes from its books.

But Southern resistance is a stubborn beast, not bound by laws. Albany schools remained segregated, as did ours. (With only Wilucia, her sister, and David as the exceptions.) Other Albany institutions and businesses took no notice of the city laws' removal.

And in Virginia's house her father, an MD, was not happy to see Virginia's outspokenness creeping into his practice, costing him patients.

****

The Albany racial grudge-match had been going on since Reconstruction, with periods of quiet, or passive rebellion, interrupted by more active Black efforts sparked by World War I Black vets returning, and voter registration drives in the '40s and '50s.

The 1960s version Virginia was involved in had as its focus not solely lunch counters, not only bus depots, not merely schools, but the integration of the entire community. Not incremental progress, but the whole shooting match at once. It was a first in the '60s.

Sadly, and uncommonly, the town had a smart sheriff.

He went to the trouble of studying the movement's non-violent strategy and used his version to up-end it. Instead of bullwhips, firehoses, dogs, guns, and red-neck support, he used peaceful arrests and dispersed incarceration. He filled jails over the entirety of southwest Georgia. It worked, according to most accounts.

Had Birmingham Commissioner of Safety Bull Connor and Selma Sheriff Jim Clark learned something from Bull's home paper, *The Birmingham Post-Herald*, the tide in America might not have shifted in favor of civil rights. The paper claimed *the manner in which Albany's chief of police has enforced the law and maintained order has won the admiration of... thousands.*

****

The idea a kid like Virginia, from my neck of the woods, and probably with the same kind of friends, could publicly go against her family and her community put me on notice. If I wanted to, I could be better. If I wanted to. If I didn't care what people thought.

Kicking the Can

I was lucky. I was bright, and, despite our financial struggles, I was culturally middle-class. Which meant I understood both the importance of education *and* how to go about getting it. At least I thought I knew those things. But here's what I actually understood.

It was important to get an education, not for any economic advantages or intellectual enhancements it might bring, but because it was going to be my ticket out of Athens. Yet it wasn't Athens I had to get shed of.

It was Mom's expectations for me. She paid lip-service to the idea I had my own life to live, but those occasional bleats did not counteract nine years of acting out the opposite, nine years of reinforcing what those strange grown-ups told me when Dad died, *Jimmy, you've got to take care of your mother now.* Unsaid but definitely included was *and Mary Win.*

I could not separate Mom's expectations from Athens' expectations. The disadvantage of a small town. Too many people knew me as a good, role-model kind of White middle-class kid. One who would do well, and do right by his mom, despite a family tragedy.

I could not envision a future where I could live in Athens and be free to be myself, whoever I was going to turn out to be. As large as the University of Georgia was, it wasn't big enough for me to hide in. Not anonymous enough for me to shed a skin, snakelike.

(I'd seen a hometown boy come home for the ritual Georgia versus Tech football celebration, drunker than a sot. I could never have done it, been happily, exuberantly, publicly drunk in my hometown. I'd never hear the end of it. Maybe he didn't.)

Big university or not, UGA was still in Athens, where lots of people knew me, Dad, Mom, my sisters, and many of our trials and successes. And I was sensitive about what people thought of me. Probably too much so.

Most folks in town did not know about Mom's instability, or how she behaved toward her kids inside the house. She wasn't terrible, but without knowing about her depression, her trip to the looney bin, her desire to leave life behind, her confusion of her needs with ours, and the insecurity all of it bred in Caroline and me, my need to get away would seem inexplicable. Particularly in a place so steeped in history, familial connections, and topophilia.

I was lucky I lived in a university town where kids like me were expected to go on to college. And I was lucky I was smart and was recruited by out-of-state schools. Mom was right. Without a significant slathering of financial aid, I was going to be stuck in town, going to UGA, and living at home to save money, at the perceived cost of my sense of self.

This college route out of town must work for an enormous number of kids. I can't be alone in this. It allowed me to leave gracefully, without having to acknowledge to anyone the huge rift growing between Mom and me, and between the South and me.

It was a route which suited me perfectly. It allowed me to avoid conflict, hide my feelings, maintain everyone's illusions, and use good manners. What I didn't know was I was only kicking a can down a road.

I didn't comprehend that I couldn't paper over my problems forever, or that I would carry the problems with me wherever I went. They wouldn't be solved by moving. I'm sure that was the point of stories I read, but I failed to make the connection.

The other bit I thought I knew was how to get an education. Here I mistook the mechanics of getting into a good school and getting a good scholarship with the actual process of acquiring a good education. I wouldn't learn the huge difference, and the cost of not letting Madame Cole's efforts bear fruit, until I'd wasted a free ride at Columbia, and managed to graduate only by the freakiest of circumstances.

Hot Town, Summer in the City

Wedding bells. Somehow Mom and I worked together successfully at the summertime-empty high school shop to build new valances for the living room curtains. We were redecorating the house for Caroline's wedding. It was satisfying to work as a team feeding big strips of plywood into the bandsaw to make scrolled backboards. At home we worked in tandem again, padding the new-sawn plywood. Perhaps having my home-leaving settled between us provided the freedom to enjoy each other.

Caroline's wedding was large and beautiful. I walked her down the aisle, probably the only *man of the house* responsibility I'd ever thoroughly enjoyed. She asked Millie if she would come back from her new home in New Hampshire and run the guest book at the reception. It was a sweet thought on Caroline's part, pleasing to both Millie and me. And Millie went for it. Sadly, we made no progress in planning or talking about our future, or whether there was to be one.

But that summer there was other progress. The City of Athens took a grudging step forward in integrating its public facilities. I was lifeguarding at the city's Legion Pool, named for its former life as an American Legion facility. A large outdoor pool with a beautifully detailed brick wing hosting the changing rooms, equipment room, and admission and concession room on one side and a generous wooden-covered, open-air sitting area making an L with the brick wing.

Part of my duties included a few days of prep before the pool opened. I was surprised when I got there the last morning to find Earl, my boss, already there and taking down the diving board. I loved our board. Though it was old and not adjustable, it had the spring of a high-jumper and a good feel. I helped him lift it off the carriage and carry it into the equipment room and asked, *Earl, why are we taking down the board?*

Because they don't have a board at the colored pool, so if we don't have one here either, they won't wanna come here.

Oh, I said out loud. Thinking to myself, *That board has a waiting line almost all the time, almost every day, so we're going to deprive everybody of one our best features in the hope a few Black kids won't come? How short-sighted and narrow-minded can we be?* But, true to form, I didn't voice the thought.

The pool opened the next morning. The first two kids into the pool were Black. In fact, the only two kids in the pool were Black. Usually on opening day there was a line out the admission door and over into the sitting area. No doubt, word was out that integration was in.

I was the sole guard on duty for the morning shift, sitting in one of those high old guard-chairs, with my life-ring on the side, and the reaching pole below me. Watching a big pool with only two kids in it and no diving board is boring. (Boards are high accident areas, so you need to scan them more frequently, and better-staffed pools have a guard dedicated to the board area.) Having the board actually kept our guards more alert.

After a while, when the two boys were near the guard chair teasing me, I cannon-balled them. Definitely a no-no. If they had done it, I would have warned them, and the next time they did it they would have been out of the water for fifteen minutes; if there was another time, sent home, no refund.

But they were so surprised it was worth it. No one else had come since they had arrived, and Earl was in the admissions room, so I was in the clear. They weren't going to tell; they didn't know the rules yet. Instead, they grabbed hold and tried to dunk me. I was bigger and a better swimmer and I dragged them around the pool instead.

Most kids loved horseplay in the water. As a guard I allowed it as long as it didn't get too rough or involve bullying. These kids were of the loved-it stripe. So, we continued for a while. Then I thought I needed to re-establish myself as the guard, so I shook them off, climbed out of the pool, and back onto my perch.

They kept on swimming and playing. Meanwhile three more potential customers came—a White woman and two tow-headed boys—but they didn't come in. They simply stood, wistful and forlorn, against the chain-link fence separating them from the pool deck. I jumped back into the pool with the Black boys and dragged them around the pool some more and got out as time drew near shift change.

When I was off duty, the woman beckoned me over to the fence.

Aren't you afraid of catching something? she wondered respectfully, as if guards were somebody to look up to.

No, Ma'am, I'm not.

She seemed like she wanted to say something more, or ask something more, but she couldn't quite get it out. I knew the feeling, but I couldn't think of what to say either.

That night, as I lay awake in bed, I could think of plenty I should have said. *It's a great day to be in the pool. It isn't crowded. I don't think there is anything to worry about regarding diseases. And if you're worried anyway, we keep the pool heavily chlorinated, and everyone is required to shower before getting in. As a last step, to get out of the changing room you have to wade through an extra-chlorinated footbath.*

I could have been a lot more reassuring. I could have added I would have the relief guard keep a special eye out for her boys.

I also thought through what I had made of the woman, probably the boys' mom. At first. I thought she was bigoted and ignorant, and her question was more of a comment on my loose behavior than a question. But I came around to thinking her attitude and question sprang from someone who was new to the pool and hadn't known that today was integration day.

It was an ignorant question, true, but it might well have been honestly intended. She would have been brought up as I was, with fears like hers surrounding her, and maybe this was her first attempt to question one.

I could have done better about helping her with her questions, and her boys would have been a lot happier in the pool rather than just staring at it. Maybe they would have played with the other boys, something

171

I never could do when I was their age. Maybe I was creating a magical kingdom in my mind, but I might have missed an opportunity there.

11. The Big Apple

Dead White Men and the GD Boy

Columbia unabashedly plagiarized the University of Chicago's approach to the first two years of a liberal arts education.

The series of small, discussion-based seminars exploring undergirding works in western literature, philosophy, history, music, and art were exactly like I thought an Ivy education should be. They went down like barbeque and coleslaw.

Although later fairly criticized as being almost exclusively a perusal of dead White men's work, the approach seemed tailored for me. Had it continued, my academic career might have unfolded differently.

****

My presence at Columbia was courtesy not only of Tom Harrold, but also of the college's geographical distribution policy. GD boys were a distinct minority. Often recognized by our not-from-New-York accents. Some people saw the GD admissions policy (favoring students from outside the New York City region) as an anti-Semitic ploy, to keep the college from becoming too Jewish. I didn't know about the controversy, and I assumed, wrongly, I would have gotten in if I hadn't been poorish and a Southerner. I was glad to be there and far away from home.

I thought it made sense to want a diverse student body. I was certainly happy to be around people different from what I was used to. It's strange now, fifty years later, to hear the value of a diverse campus being disputed.

I missed a couple of clues, however, about facing challenges. In high school I had underestimated the difference between recreational swimming and competitive swimming, and it took me a year of hard work to catch up.

Unfortunately, it didn't become a life-lesson for jumping from Georgia public school to the Ivy League. Madame Cole tried to show me an alternative to gliding through school, but I didn't think about changing.

I didn't believe the jump to an Ivy college was going to require higher levels of skill, training, and natural ability than I had. But Columbia had also adopted Chicago's approach to GD students once they reached campus. Fly, die, or struggle.

I was pushing blasé to new heights.

A Different Kind of Canoe

When I registered for Columbia courses the first time, I disdained Poet's Math, the pre-calc course. I figured it was for people with math problems.

I didn't comprehend the level of my fellow students. At Columbia, a guy from Georgia public schools who had soared through all the math courses available (which certainly did not include pre-calculus or calculus) was, almost by definition, a guy with math problems. My advisor didn't question me when I signed up for calculus. He should have.

And my own limitations worked against me too. First, I couldn't admit how far out of my depth I was in calculus once I got into it, and second, I didn't believe anybody could help. Which left me devouring the literature, art, and philosophy/history courses, while floundering and flailing in calculus like a lifeguard mimicking a drowner. (Though drowners often go down without a whimper.)

It didn't help that it was my first experience with a mass lecture course, and that it was staged in a staggering amphitheater. I was intimidated by the setting alone.

****

Here's another clue I failed to catch. Freshman orientation week, despite my expressed delight in being happy around people different from me, I was hanging out with other GD boys from Texas and Utah. We were on the plaza for recruitment day, the day when clubs and sports and activities publicize themselves and try to lure new freshmen into their ranks.

We were standing near a long and slender canoe, listening to someone talk about some sport or other, when my new friend Rip started admiring the boat.

Boy, I've never seen anything like it.

Me neither.

The hull glistened, and its insides reminded me of vintage Old Town wood and canvas boats, but thinner with a narrower beam and strip planking.

Some kids behind us, dressed in slacks and sport shirts, with sweaters looped around their necks, overheard Rip's confession of ignorance, tapped him on the back, and quizzed him, incredulously, *My God, man! Where did you prep?*

The tapper was a crew jock, and we were studying their racing shell.

I learned during my first semester what a prep school was and that these boys had to have been preppies. Later I learned their attire was already becoming cliché. But I also learned many of them had acquired a comprehensive and rigorous education, and they actually studied.

175

I hadn't begun to recognize that hitting the books and note-taking at a rigorous level was necessary, much less how to do it. This encounter on the plaza could have been a *Toto, I've a feeling we're not in Kansas anymore* moment. But I remained unready to change and adapt.

Call Home

A year and a half later I knew I was in trouble. The tin-can I had kicked down the road wouldn't go any further. Now it sat on me and grew ominously large and jagged. Phone calls home were grim duties doused in withheld pain and stiff awkwardness. I had nothing to say to Mom, nor she to me, but she needed the contact. I was grudging in giving it.

The dorm phone system didn't make it easier. We had one phone per floor and calls were routed through a switchboard downstairs. Incoming calls were picked up by anybody on the floor willing to be bothered. After answering they went yelling up and down the floor shouting for the intended recipient. The phone was in the dingy hall, three steps away from the shower room. An unpromising and unfailingly bleak setting for any conversation; yet fitting for my calls from home.

****

Academically I was OK but no star. Otherwise, I was hurting.

The extreme changes I had blithely sought out were traumatic. New York's foreignness never became a comfortable background, and the unacknowledged size of the break with my mother blocked me emotionally.

Keeping secret the scope of the break drained me. The unexpectedly higher level of academic competition stomped my ego, and my inability to let go of Millie or go forward with her consumed me. I was a mess.

Other than that, everything was fine.

Oh yeah, except… my study habits were still below what was needed, I had no sense of how to seek out teachers or anyone else for advice and guidance, and no one stepped forward to take on the role as Madame Cole had.

I wasn't flunking out, but the joy of those initial great books courses was fading fast. By the next year, it was gone for good.

I had accomplished the one goal in life I had—departing home. After leaving, I was spent, unwilling to contemplate returning home, uneasy in the City, unable to consider quitting and going to work, and willfully ignorant of the Vietnam draft consequences if I did make a radical change.

Football saved me.

Lightweight

As bad as the team was, I loved playing ball.

Our shoulder pads were stamped *Irregular*; a tetanus shot came with the physical because the field was watered with untreated Harlem River water; the coach was an alcoholic who only held his job because nobody cared; my helmet broke on a hard hit in scrimmage; and we only knew how to run half of our offense.

But I enjoyed every bit of contact. I was pissed about many things, and if I couldn't articulate the anger or deal with it in any other way, football gave me an outlet I knew how to use.

Welcome to Columbia Lightweight Football.

****

Part of Tom Harrold's pitch for Columbia was I could play ball there. They had two varsity teams. The one every Ivy had with big, but smart,

177

guys, and Columbia's unknown team, with little, but smart, guys—the lightweight squad—one hundred fifty-four pounds maximum. Tom didn't mention both teams were terrible. It wouldn't have fazed me if he had.

If anything, the opportunity to play football again loomed brighter in my imagination than my thoughts about *making the biggest change possible*. It's what we don't admit to anyone that makes a difference.

Suiting up again. Blocking and tackling. Getting sweaty and dirty, wearied and bruised. That's what I thought about, the images which were neon-vivid and gave me the strength I needed. Needed to hold tight my decision to leave family and culture for the land of the enemy. Mom, of course, knew nothing about this.

****

For no good reason, only hubris, I assumed I would make the lightweight football team as a walk-on who hadn't played since eighth grade. I would have no concerns about breaking Mom's heart, since I would continue my silence. The reach of my fantasy was broad. I would make the team. And I would start. I would never get hurt. And Mom would never know any of it.

On the day we first turned out, guys showed up whose fantasies exceeded mine. Guys who brought their own helmets from the dime store. Guys who insisted on playing in sneakers—no cleats. Guys who had never played any ball. And everybody made the team. I hadn't known it was a no-cut proposition. You might not play, but you wouldn't get cut from the squad. A good way to treat people.

Though we turned out for ball our freshman year, we weren't eligible to play on the team. Another surprise. What we were able to do was play *against* the team as their practice opposition. My eyes got opened. They blew right past me. They were so quick. So disciplined and sharp. We, the

178

freshmen, were shown exactly what we were — slow meat. Some, not me, had played high school ball. Some of those were good. The rest of us had a lot of drills to get through.

Sophomore year, some of my fantasy came true. I made the starting offense as a blocking back. Every offensive play, with only one exception, I was to hit people, that is, to block them. As forcefully as possible. Using my body as a wrecking ball. My dream job.

Somebody comes toward my quarterback, I pop them. Somebody comes for my running back, I pop them. Simple, straightforward, easy to understand, easy to do, and so enjoyable. Social value? None. Anger-management tool? Off the charts.

The one exception to my blocking role was a short-yardage pass play, where I rolled downfield ten yards, juked left, and cut to the right sideline. I was supposedly the primary pass receiver. I rarely was, but there's a reason. I dropped balls in practice. Never in a game. But too often in practice. The quarterback got gun-shy about throwing them my way.

An example: we were playing Navy in Annapolis. They were tough. Every midshipman had to play at least one sport, and their lightweight team could have given some heavyweight college teams a good game. (In contrast, my Columbia lightweight team got beaten by high schools.)

The stands were full, and the Navy crowd stood for the entire game. It was like being in an alternate universe. No one even *came* to our home games.

We were only behind two touchdowns when our quarterback called my play. I ran my route downfield, made my fake inside, and cut to the outside. I was open! Throw the ball! I saw the quarterback's eyes. He was looking everywhere but at me. I kept running for the sideline. The defensive back caught up with me. We were going stride for stride. Then he was joined by what seemed like the whole Navy team.

Finally, and I swear I could see the resignation in his eyes, my quarterback threw the ball toward me and my Navy buddies. I jumped like

179

I was both blocking out and rebounding on the basketball floor, and somehow touched the ball. I grabbed it, cradled it, and was rolled under by a massive, moving wall of seamen. I was down, but I had the ball for a short gain.

I never saw the ball again for the rest of the game. But nobody sacked my quarterback either.

The Stalker and the River

By spring semester of my sophomore year, I had abandoned my clean-cut guise and roamed the campus and the city in a tattered khaki field jacket of Dad's, complementing my raggedy jeans and unkempt long hair. Sometimes I searched for Dad in downtown crowds or on the subway. I pretended nothing was odd, and that I was OK, but the sore parts of my head and heart told me otherwise. Once I thought I saw someone who might be him. I followed him for a bit.

I knew it couldn't be Dad, but there was that thought. I didn't stop following because I knew it was stupid, or because I knew it was strange. I broke off because I didn't want to find out it wasn't him.

****

Surprising myself, I sought some help. I went to one of the school counselors.

This was the first time I'd reached for any kind of help since my days with Kelley, and it was rare then. Dr. Medalie asked me why I was so scruffy. I took the question as criticism, because criticism was what it would have been at home. But now I think she actually wanted to know, because she thought it would help her, and me, understand me. No way could I answer that.

No way could I tell her the tattered jacket had been Dad's, and it was my tie to him and a time when my family was whole. Or, I was scruffy because I had been so clean-cut all my life, and was in trite rebellion. Or, how completely I was lost. How I didn't understand a school without girls. And I didn't know how to study, or what I wanted to study when I finished the required core courses.

Much less that I had abandoned my church, struggled with its belief system, and thought I shouldn't preach (even if I got my faith straightened out) unless it was more meaningful than me holding forth because I liked to show off. That I had no idea what I wanted to do with my life. That I wasn't in college to learn but to escape home.

And I was haunted by my decision to leave. I was supposed to take care of Mom. I was supposed to take care of Mary Win. I had received the message less than subtly from Mom and more graciously from my community. But I ran away from those responsibilities and had run into a foreign land. I couldn't go home and admit defeat, and here I couldn't find my way.

At our fourth meeting, I told her a little bit about it. I told her of a dream I'd had. It wasn't a recurring dream but was powerfully surreal. The leading character was the Oconee. I took the dream to mean that although I felt deeply and damagingly guilty about abandoning my family, there was no guarantee if I had stayed, their life would work out better. Caroline had already married and left the family nest, and who knew what was in store for Mom and Mary Win, whether I was there or not.

I couldn't explain the Oconee to her, much less my own life, but I told her the Oconee was an ugly, polluted river surrounding the town and it was the dream-driver. I couldn't go deeper then, and I certainly couldn't tell her what I've written here.

I couldn't let her in on how odd it was, since Athens and the river were inseparable, that I should have such strong feelings about the light, beauty, and supportive grace of the town and such disquieting feelings

181

about the river's threat. And how revealing it was that in this dream, eleven years from when our family life fell apart, and two years from when I made my choice to leave, it was the river which forced me to examine my choice.

And surprisingly, in its bleakness, the dream-river gave me a glimmer of a new, more forgiving, less damning understanding of the choice I'd made.

When I made the choice to leave, it seemed like I had to do it. If I accepted my stay-at-home fate, I would abandon whatever potential I had and lose myself in the *dutiful son* persona carefully constructed for me, and by me.

Despite having stood by my choice to leave, I nonetheless felt I had betrayed my responsibility. Both my religion and my family believed in sacrifice. I did too.

But the dream opened up a bleak, but ultimately more merciful, way of understanding my decision.

I thought of the dream as a poem, and in my sophomoric way I transcribed it.

It is the light of twilight,
Or early in a sunless day,
Yet there is no morning or evening.

It is timeless.

My mother, sisters, and I float in the river.
Father is gone,
But not missing,
The family is complete.

Immersing, the water does not wet us.

Neither warm nor cold,
It is only the river.

Familiar, enveloping, distant.

We float with no effort,
Our heads buoyed,
No sense of our bodies.

Not without bodies, but bodies without importance.

This river of filth does not smell.
Rustier than usual, but I know this river,
The river of my childhood.

It frightens me.

It moves us steadily,
But there are no drops.
Bare skeletal oaks alone mark our passage.

Mary Win is missing.

I stop, look back,
and she recedes.
But without looking,

I know Mother and Caroline have not stopped.

Mary Win is frail.
Torn,

I wait for her.

In an instant she is gone.

I turn for Mother
And Caroline.
They are gone.

I am alone,
In a gray world,
In the river of decay.

I am lost.

Church for Church

The Wretched Twig, Danny, and Spence—all GD boys from Texas, Spence already a licensed Baptist lay-preacher—made a deal with me.

They would come to Riverside Church with me and hear the visiting Reverend Dr. Martin Luther King, Jr., preach. But only if I came to Marble Collegiate Church and listened with them to Dr. Norman Vincent Peale, pastor of the church and author of the self-help tome *The Power of Positive Thinking.*

I pounced on the proposition. I wasn't thrilled about Peale—I thought (without having read or heard anything by him) positive thinking was a shallow approach to life's challenges. I liked to keep a smile on, but I knew there was heartache and tragedy loose in the world.

However, the idea of going to hear King with some guys from the same background sparked a hopeful warmth in me, and Peale was a small price to pay. These would be the first times I had been to church since I

184

left home (barring some required peace-keeping missions when in Athens).

It was spring of 1967, and while I imagined I had fully embraced the civil rights movement, I wasn't sure about my friends. Some exposure to Dr. King in person might be good for all of us.

None of us heard about civil rights the way we expected. Not because of our racist pasts. Not because we were challenged to change our beliefs and our actions regarding Black people. But because Dr. King preached on Vietnam.

I don't remember a single word of his eloquence. Not his painting of Vietnam as *the symptom of a far deeper malady within the American spirit.* Not his prophecy that if we didn't change our hearts and our course, *we shall surely be dragged down the long, dark, and shameful corridors of time reserved for those who possess power without compassion, might without morality, and strength without sight.*

But I got a message. Dr. King was telling us our country's treatment of Black Americans was not separate from our treatment of Vietnam, and not separate from our acceptance of persistent poverty either. They were linked.

He foresaw in our future there would be marches and rallies *without end unless there is a significant and profound change in American life and policy. So, such thoughts take us beyond Vietnam, but not beyond our calling as sons of the living God.*

****

Twig asked me as we left the church, *What'd you think?*

The message I got, still wrestling with the war myself, and not usually the first one to discern the arc of justice bending, *I think he should stick to civil rights.*

185

****

The next week at Marble Collegiate, Dr. Peale was predictably bland, and I took nothing away. Twig didn't bother to ask.

A Ride

Hankering for freedom, adventures, mobility, and possessing a certain lack of prudence, I bought a motorcycle.

A Columbia senior didn't feel he would need it in his upcoming life and offered an attractive price. Five hundred dollars, which I actually had, for a seven-year-old BMW 500.

Caroline and her husband got me started on bikes when they were newly married. They acquired a step-through Honda 50 they both rode. I progressed with them through their Hondas. First the 50, then the 90, ending with their 160. Their progression continued, but alas, not in Athens.

Five hundred dollars for 500 ccs and the Beemer badge was irresistible. BMW bikes ruled an obscure racing class.

12. Back in Athens

Sam

That summer I tried to get out on a merchant marine ship. The fruitless time I spent in the National Maritime Union hiring hall was tedious boredom interrupted by rare moments of fascinating brilliance.

In the hall there were two others like me, inexperienced youngsters in the lowest seniority class. One was a beefy blond kid who fancied himself tough. The other was scragglier than I was and longer-haired. He made himself a target by ignoring the chairs available and sitting on the floor with his back to the wall. Sometimes playing a wooden flute.

The three of us were each waiting for a berth to get knocked down to our classification, the Group Fours.

Blondie smelled blood, and kept picking at Scraggly, finally goading him into accepting a fight. But it didn't go according to plan.

Not that Scraggly was a martial arts black belt. Something better. A dark and wiry young mariner marched both of them off the property before they squared off. Outside it was one-sided, and he was the one.

No fighting in the hall! This is a brotherhood. If you've got a legitimate beef take it to the steward. If you don't, stow it. Now shake hands.

And then back to tedium. (But I carried *For the Union Makes Us Strong* music and sentiments into the hall with me.)

While Blondie laid off Scraggly.

****

Time, patience, and money were running low as I waited for a berth. I gave up and ran the bike back to Athens.

There I spent the rest of the summer working construction on a university classroom building. I was lucky to get a job late in the summer, but they were short on laborers. I toted, hauled, pushed, dug, shoveled, pounded, hammered, broomed, and, once, waded into murky water to rescue equipment and salvage rebar-work.

The other college guy and I were the only ones on the labor crew accepting the foreman's request for volunteers to leap in and set the site right following a towering no-notice thunderstorm. The deluge turned our site into a swimming hole, and the older guys had more sense than to blindly jump into the campus's new murky-brown pool.

In a surprise ending we got out unharmed, the compactors we hauled out undamaged, and the rebar cages secured and straightened.

Sam, a sweet older laborer, came over with some not-too-dirty rags to dry with. He wanted to know if we'd seen any snakes. We hadn't. But it was only then we grasped we could have. One of the reasons no one else volunteered. Another reason came to me later. The company couldn't order any of us to go in. It was a safety and pay issue.

No one knew if it would be safe or not, so the foreman couldn't order anyone in without extra compensation. Our youthful sense of adventure might have cost someone extra pay they could have used.

Sam came immediately to mind. He wore well-cared-for but well-used faded blue bib overalls, farmer-style. And he was noticeably thinner than anyone else on the site. Not only was he the only guy among the laborers beyond middle-age, but he was well-worn. Like older guys on a labor gang are. Over the years laboring takes a lot out of the body, replacing what it's taken with pain.

There was another aspect of Sam which struck me. He wore an

old-school round shiny metal hard-hat. The rest of us were in the more recent generation of white plastic, ball-cap-shaped hats. Sam clearly owned his own. It had his name on it, carefully hand-painted.

****

The laborers ate together on a shady grass bank right outside the site fence. I sometimes brought a book to read, and Sam seemed interested that I read for fun. I thought about saying something about the lettering on his hat, thinking about how he might appreciate some help with reading, but I wouldn't ask with the other guys around.

And Sam seemed proud of his hat. It seemed there was no good way to broach the subject. Hard not to seem condescending or critical. I let it lie.

Sam was Black and none of the rest of us were. It was possible to weave his Blackness into the narrative about him growing in my head, but I found it impossible without wondering how much my racist stereotypes were driving the story.

A better idea might have been to have a genuine conversation with him, if he were willing, and let him tell me his story himself.

A Road Not Taken

My bike had acquired a few wounds under my care. One of the first lessons you learn leaving New York via motorbike is not to drive near the center of a lane exiting a toll-plaza. Goose the gas and you're going fish-tailing down the highway in the oil and grease left behind by a million leaky cars.

I was lucky. I stayed upright. And it was pretty impressive. There were other times, though, when my inexperience cost us both. I got some road rash here and there and the BMW lost its medallion. To make up for the loss, I added a big ding to the gas tank.

At home in Athens, I couldn't reach into the tank to bang it out, so I filled the oversized dimple with bondo — body filler — and repainted it flat black. The missing marquee badge and the oddly repainted tank confused people about the bike's pedigree. Made it more dangerous looking.

I flailed my funkcycle to the construction site every morning and back home to Cloverhurst every evening. Still too young to drink in Georgia, I sometimes stopped off at The Shack drive-in, a college dive near the construction site, for a Coke and fries. Too dirty to go inside. Too tired to want to go home. Too bored to do anything else.

****

Except for the occasional cloudburst, it was always hot. Pushing, and controlling, a wheelbarrow full-up with 800 pounds of sloppy wet concrete took a lot out of me. The motorcycle ride home from a day working construction turned the sweat into a cooling breeze.

Riding shirtless to the Shack, wearing my hardhat instead of my helmet one afternoon, I noticed a VW Bug on my tail. The Bug burped and I pulled over, wondering what was up. A guy about my age, maybe a little older, clambered out of the VW and nervously gingered up beside my bike.

You interested in making some money? Sure, I shot back, wondering what the job would be. *Can you meet me out at the small motel on the Watkinsville Highway? You know where it is? Yeah, I've been out there a time or two.* Both the big motel and the little motel were owned by friends' families. Classmates had standing invitations to come out and use the pools. The smaller one also pastured our friend's Shetland pony. His early birthday parties were held there and included rides on the pony. So, yeah, I knew where it was.

So you know what I'm talking about, then? I didn't.

But, on second thought, I did.

Thinking *Oh. My answer about being out at the motel a couple of times was probably misleading.* I hastened to clear matters up, saying *I do now. I didn't at first. And no, thank you. I thought you had a home improvement project or something like that. Sorry for the misunderstanding.* He said only *Thanks* and walked back to his Bug.

I sat there on the bike till he was gone, surprised at myself.

I was pleased he thought I was hot.

Michigan

Mom and I got along well enough that summer to plan an expedition together. We'd travel to the palm of the mitten state and visit her Michigan sisters and brother who stayed close to where they were born. We'd drive her Dodge Dart, hauling the motorcycle on a rental trailer, and I'd part company with her and Mary Win after visiting a while with my cousins, uncles, and aunts.

After the visiting, I'd take the bike and head back to New York through Canada, crossing back into the US at Niagara Falls, and continuing along the path of the Erie Canal till I hit Interstate 87 going south with the Hudson River. The deciduous leaves would still be green in the forests, about a month shy of their showy metamorphosis, and there were plenty of campgrounds along the route. I'd see a big swath of new country.

Somewhat to my surprise, I enjoyed the trip north with Mom and Mary Win, and delighted in renewing friendships with my cousins. But they didn't understand how I could live in New York City. On my part, I couldn't admit there were downsides. I also chose not to express my opinion some of them might want to get out and explore a bit more of the world.

191

In the comfort of family, I forgot my appearance was much different than theirs. And that my long hair and behemoth black bike might make an over-scale, not altogether favorable, impression on my kin. The hair and bike were, at the least, intriguing. The topic still comes up occasionally.

****

I like my relatives, but Aunt Bel—who came to stay with us kids when Mom went away—is the one who left a big impression on me this visit. I had started smoking, at first to learn to inhale so I could get the benefit from the marijuana abounding in New York, but also because I thought it was manly. I didn't indulge around Mom or Mary Win, or in our house, but I had the Marlboros around. I kept one pack in the glove compartment of the Dart.

Driving Aunt Bel and Mary Win out to my Aunt Dee's farm to pick Mom up from a visit, I asked Aunt Bel to please get my sunglasses for me out of the glovebox, forgetting entirely about the cigs therein.

She saw them, turned around to Mary Win in the back seat and exclaimed, *Mary Win, I didn't know you smoked!*

Mary Win was puzzled, and before she could reply I owned up, abashed. *Those are mine, Aunt Bel.*

She had treated my sister like a real person. A person with will and an agency of her own. I was always shocked when someone treated her normally—which wasn't often. And it always made me wish I thought like they did.

13. Return to Gotham

Niagara Falls, Ontario

I rolled into the plaza by the falls in early evening. I was tired, wet, and excited. There was so much noise from the dropping water, and so much mist from the dropping water, it was like being inside a soft thunderstorm. The sound found a way to my innards and I started resonating with the roar. Uumming, almost shaking.

Maybe the aftermath of a long bike ride was also in play.

I admired the falls a long time. Walking downstream hip-to-guardrail to get a better view, and back upstream to where I had parked the bike close to the lip. Two Harleys pulled in and parked next to me.

Harley owners often look down on other bikes, particularly Japanese ones, and more particularly two-stroke Japanese bikes. Fortunately, my German-made four-stroke had some cachet of its own.

And despite the failing light, the missing BMW badge, the poorly repaired gas tank, and the general lack of spit and polish, they recognized the bike for what it was. A good road-bike, whose opposed cylinders and shaft-drive dampened drive-train noise and vibration. I chatted with the hogs' owners — they too were from the States — and smothered any expression of my delight about being accepted into the biker fraternity with no questions, or demeaning remarks about the character of my ride.

It was a high point, but certainly could raise questions about who I thought I was, and who was I trying to impress.

Niagara Falls, New York

I crossed back into the US without a problem. A driver's license and no questions. Nineteen sixty-seven, pre-9/11. Over the Rainbow Bridge, sneaking glances upstream to the floodlit Falls and the shimmery multi-hued arc, I found a motel with the vacancy light on near the river.

Everything was fine until the desk clerk saw my helmet. *We don't take bikers.* I wanted to argue, but he wasn't budging. Besides I couldn't say *I'm not a biker. I'm just a college student masquerading.* He had the law on his side anyway. Bikers aren't a protected class.

Pissed as I was, the refusal of service did make me think. I could clean my appearance up and drive a car. Changes I could make. I didn't have to change my skin.

3940 Broadway

It was a jolt. Walking carefully in an unfamiliar, perhaps hostile, neighborhood and suddenly thinking I recognized the spot.

Am I standing kitty-corner from the Audubon Ballroom? Where Malcom X was assassinated in 1965?

Vista Volunteer Mike, my mentor, assured me I was. We were past Harlem, standing on the corner of 165th and Broadway in Washington Heights.

The notoriety of our location brought home to me how out of place I was. One of two White guys walking in tandem and cold-knocking on doors, like lost Mormon missionaries.

While I had spruced myself up to come here—I was working with Mike in a fitful effort to help the city reduce its drug problems—I couldn't clean-up enough for anyone to mistake me for a Mormon. Too much hair.

194

Normally I dressed in over-worn jeans and a shapeless sweatshirt with stretched-out cuffs and neckband. Working the streets with Mike, I wore laundered chinos and a lightly starched collared shirt. A style lost somewhere between working-class street and Southern prep.

My wardrobe shift didn't help our success rate and couldn't improve my obvious honkiness. The neighborhood wasn't Black and it wasn't Brown and it wasn't Jewish. It was those and more.

Myself, I naturally exuded hopelessly Anglo-Protestant genetics which weren't welcome. Mike did the talking. At least he was Jewish.

****

We weren't truly cold knocking; we had a list of names and addresses from NYC's Addiction Services Agency. And everybody on the list had a relative with a drug problem. Maybe Mike knew how the city knew. I didn't. Probably courts or probation.

We were supposed to organize the people who were willing to open their doors into support groups and transform the support groups into activist hives for their community.

Most doors wouldn't grudge a crack. Mike had one such group of relatives alive but on life-support in East Harlem before I joined him. This week we were in unplowed, obviously infertile territory trying to get another group started.

In the Heights, the few doors opening were backed by women. She could be Jewish, Greek, Soviet, Cuban, Afro-American, Puerto Rican, or Dominican. But usually a first- or second-generation immigrant. If we were lucky, she would speak English and Mike could give his spiel in our native tongue. If they spoke Spanish, Mike could almost manage. Slowly. All else was towering babble.

In any language it would be a tough sell. *We're here from the City. We understand your husband is in jail on a drug charge. There are many women in this neighborhood with a similar problem; would you like to meet with some of them to talk about how to deal with the problem?*

The same city that was jailing their loved ones was showing up at their doorsill, uninvited, offering help by encouraging them to talk with complete strangers. How about a good lawyer instead? Or some rent money? Or bail money? Or cops that came when you called?

I was surprised more doors didn't slam in our faces.

Therapeutic Community

I was turned loose on the streets of New York courtesy of my work-study award.

Having spent two years in food service working my way up from busboy to cashier, I was bored. And I wanted something more involved with life in the community.

Columbia hooked me up with the newly established city Addiction Services Agency. I would start by sitting in on encounter groups with a bunch of detoxing junkies at the Morris J. Bernstein Institute, downtown at 18th Street and 2nd Avenue. With the work-hours left-over I would canvass with Mike.

A lecture from the head of the agency, a handout, and the sessions at the institute would be it for training and introduction. Mike would clue me in on the rest as we worked. No heads up that Mike hadn't been on the streets long and had only the same minimal background I had. Also, no warning the therapy groups were highly confrontational, loud, and emotional. Rationality was not highly prized.

****

I rolled downtown on the bike. When I found my way to the group, I was a minute or so late. It was like being a living football practice-dummy.

Everybody took a shot at me.

There were eleven junkies in the group and one straight—me. The leader was a detoxed user. The program had a reward and punishment structure underlying the operation, and leadership roles were both rewards and training for life outside.

The program also had a strong belief it was easier for a junkie to listen to another junkie than to some non-doper do-gooder. With the social-worker and medical types, addicts could dissemble using the excuse *You don't know what I'm going through.*

In street language, you can't bullshit a bullshitter, you can't con a con, and it takes one to know one.

It was in groups that I got my first hint of the delights and freedom which a foul mouth can provide.

****

When the dopers got through grilling me about *Why the hell are you here?* and *Who the hell do you think you are?* they took to confronting me about trying to be a tough-guy with my motorcycle and black leather jacket—they could see right through me. *Come on*, they challenged me, *dress down. Lose the leather jacket. Lose the big hair. Stop posing.*

They had a point. I knew it. But I wasn't going to give in. I'm stubborn. And I wouldn't yell at them to shut up and leave me alone either. Wouldn't do what they wanted me to do. And I damn sure wouldn't cry. But yeah, I wanted to yell like them. Let it all hang out.

Get the hell off my back. I'm not the one stuck here trying to get done with dope, Goddammit! I love my bike, and I love my jacket, and I love having some wheels to get around in this goddamn city. And I don't have a clue what the hell is going on, and I'm not too proud to admit it. So why doesn't somebody

197

let me know why I'm here, and what the hell I'm supposed to do when I'm out with Mike walking the streets uptown?

I wasn't going to get honest and loud for a couple of years yet.

The attack pack moved on. Getting to me was the point, with me dropping my guard and letting myself go the goal. That was the therapeutic part. Because dropping your guard is when you reveal yourself. But I hate being set-up. I refuse to play. Mom did it to me too many times.

I refuse to play even if it would do me well. But I didn't grasp any of that then. Not the group dynamic, nor my own motivations.

Nor the idea I couldn't grow inside the shells I was layering on.

****

I was only the opening act. Al, a neat, bald, compact Black guy, was the main attraction. The leader nodded at him, and Al told his story. A sad one. He had been a rising star in the program. It went something like this.

By last weekend I had earned Friday and Saturday out on my own. I had been clean two months, and I hadn't fucked up anything inside. I was ramrodding for the maintenance crew and had it running well.

But I screwed up. I went out with my old friends Saturday night, and they got high. I told them I didn't want to join, but they went ahead. I didn't leave.

That didn't sound like a big deal to me. If you could believe him, and I did, he had resisted the temptation to use any drugs, and when he came back, he explained what he'd done.

But the rest of encounter group was shouting. *What the fuck were you thinking?? You can't hang out with your old friends! You know it. You'd risk all those drug-free weeks just to please some other dope-fiends!? We looked up to you, Goddammit! Did you ever think of that?*

198

Everybody's voice trying to climb over everyone else's.

You're gonna start right back at the bottom. And you're telling us you didn't have a taste? Not even a little taste!?

Al waited till the pack took a communal breath. *I fucked up. It was a mistake. I came back here as soon as I realized I wasn't ready to go back outside.*

More outbursts from the group. *You put the whole program at risk, you idiot! You never thought of that, did you! What if you got busted?* But the steam was running out.

It had been a startling introduction to the encounter group process, and Al's ballsy confession imprinted on my brain.

And made me appreciate why the rules were so strict. The slide backwards was too easy.

****

Junkies had, according to three different schools of thought, either a disease, a moral failure, or a lack of will. Any of which could be fatal—sudden or prolonged—through OD, shooting by police, shooting by other junkies or dealers, knifing, freezing, starving, or a multiplicity of drug-abuse-related diseases.

The overly hot debate about root causes haunts addiction services. As I'm writing in the late twenty-teens, it's getting in the way of dealing with the latest drug crisis—an opioid epidemic.

Why, with so many different people affected, should there be only one right approach? Especially since the most consistent root cause is politicians who prefer prohibition over legalization and punishment over treatment. Despite overwhelming evidence, treatment is more effective and costs less. And the punishments? Always landing disproportionately on people and families of color.

****

Al grasped he was lucky. The new program at Morris Bernstein was giving him a realistic shot at getting clean and staying clean. Not everyone in the little trial group was going to hold that belief. Some were simply marking time.

Al's stand-up response impressed me. On my part I wasn't sure if our situations had been reversed, I could have made the decision he did.

I am sure, however, that in the reversed roles, Al would have had the strength to cop to the truth about hiding behind the motorcycle and leather jacket image. Almost labeled cured, he was willing to start over at the bottom, to make sure he got it right.

14. Mistakes Were Made

Others First

I made my own mistakes in 1968. But I wasn't the only one screwing up.

President Johnson and his advisors had massively transposed a minor key regional independence struggle into the major key US-Vietnam War. It wasn't hard to do if you consistently lied to the US public about what you were doing, what the outcome would be, and what the price could be.

****

With 1968, a new phase is now starting. We have reached an important point when the end begins to come into view. Gen. William Westmoreland.

And President Johnson, answering the monster question *How long would the war continue?* With straight face, from the flight deck of the aircraft carrier USS *Enterprise*, while North Vietnam prepared the Tet attacks - *Not many more nights.*

At the Personal Level

I quit football.

In pre-season scrimmage I took a bad hit. My body went one way and my double-helixed legs went another. My right knee screamed. I was out for the rest of the scrimmage. The trainer examined the knee and said *Rest it.* That was it for diagnosis and treatment.

I laid off it until the first game. Pre-game I suited up, ran the drills (gimping a little, but not bad I thought), and prepared to start.

At the last moment the coach said, *I don't think your knee's ready to play. Sit this one out. I'm sure you'll be ready for the next one.* I didn't trust him, and the disappointment was as crushing as the hit had been. I sat the game out, but I never came back.

I missed it terribly.

I went from being lost, but having football to cling to, to being lost without a lifeline.

Rhyming History

It wasn't the first team I quit. I quit the high school swim team too. My senior year. I told people it was because I had time conflicts with my student-body presidential responsibilities. But I lied.

The truth was I lost a race in practice to a new underclassman swimmer. I had given it every bit I had, barely swallowing my vomit at the end, but he out-touched me at the wall. I couldn't stand it, and I gave up the team when practice ended.

I grew up with Kelley's Good Thought Notebook and its *Winners never quit; Quitters never win* simplicity, and I believed in it. But I quit anyway. After I quit (no announcement, no fanfare, simply didn't come to practice anymore), the coach never asked why. My friends asked and got my lie back. But I knew I had handled the loss poorly.

Fate wanted to make a point, so the same year we got a new swimmer from California, where swimmers with aspirations and talent went for training. And from being a perennial second or third place team at the

202

state meet, the team won the championship. If I'd stayed on the team, I could have shared in the victory.

Seeing the team in their leather letter-jackets — for the first time the nerdy swim-team got jackets — was hard to smile at. Harder yet was nobody seemed to miss me.

****

There's no excuse for repeating the same mistake, unless you count self-destructiveness.

Cultural and Physical Geography

Columbia lives in a part of New York City's Upper West Side called Morningside Heights, sitting roughly between Riverside Park on the west, Manhattanville and Harlem at 125th Street to the north, Morningside Park and Harlem to the east, and 110th Street to the south.

Morningside Park is not flat. It rises vertically 140 feet on its western flank, making the institutions clustered at the top — Columbia, the Cathedral of St. John the Divine, Barnard College, St. Luke's Hospital — seem ivory towers come to life over Harlem.

The symbolism of the lordly institutions' physical location was not lost on the Black and Puerto Rican communities surrounding, and, for a time, part of Morningside Heights. Instead, the symbolism was reinforced by Columbia's ham-fisted, smash-and-grab attempts to gentrify the areas around her buildings and campuses during the '50s and '60s.

In the 1950s the university's takeover of residential buildings removed over 6,300 Blacks and Puerto Ricans from the area. In the '60s, over one hundred structures succumbed to Columbia's thirst for a more "us-like" environment. More white-skinned, richer, and better educated.

203

Columbia didn't intend for the litany to include *more clueless*, but it did. The administration never anticipated struggle, push-back, or a police assault.

At least for Columbia they came when called.

The Deal

In 1960, Columbia University offered a proposition to New York City. In my view, it was like offering to pick someone's pocket for them. *Tell you what, we'd like to put our new gymnasium on your underused, vertiginous, trashy city park in our neighborhood. We'll throw-in a community center for the neighborhood as part of our project. How about a fifty-year ground lease with an option to renew for another fifty? Say a nominal lease of $3,000 per year for your cliff?*

(Full disclosure: The university also promised ongoing exterior maintenance of the community center and insisted whenever the topic came up the best benefit flowing to the city was the university's fronting the cost of the new community center.)

Mayor Robert Wagner and Parks Commissioner Robert Moses (whose biographer Robert Caro called *the most racist individual I have ever met*) jumped at it, and the nearby Harlem community was supportive. But Columbia dithered, and by 1968 when Columbia and the city brought the plan back to life, times had changed.

****

What had seemed to be a win-win for everyone in 1960 looked like *Gym Crow* to the Black community by '67-'68. The same old separate and decidedly unequal segregation.

A small *Community Entrance* on the lower level closest to Harlem contrasted poorly with the proposed grand *Columbia Entrance* 140 feet above on the west, whiter, side of the neighborhood. And there was to be no access between the lower level and the upper level.

Racial consciousness had kicked up on April 4 of '68 when Martin Luther King, Jr., was assassinated. However, the Columbia trustees, Columbia's President Grayson Kirk, and Mayor Lindsay's two-year-old NYC administration failed to catch the tide. They tried to push the gym through.

The Harlem community was no longer supportive.

House Call

President Kirk, Sir, I believe you have visitors, I imagine the housekeeper saying. The West Harlem community had come calling. To his home. Bearing picket signs.

Sir, They're Back

Three months later, the West Harlem and the Morningside Heights communities both came calling. The city's Board of Estimate — responsible for city land use, as well as city budget, contracts, franchises, and water rates — had voted unanimously to allow Columbia to proceed with the gym.

Columbia student organizations, including the Student Council, the recently-formed Students' Afro-American Society (SAS), and the Columbia chapter of CORE — the Congress of Racial Equality — had been active in opposition to the gym location for several years. And these groups were coordinating with Harlem CORE and the West Harlem Community Organization.

There they were; back confronting tone-challenged, deft-touch-challenged President Grayson Kirk.

The Earth Moved

On February 19, 1968, Columbia tried using heavy yellow dozers to power its way through the park/gymnasium opposition. Shoving dirt to quick-start gym construction. The next day twelve community and student protestors blocked the site-work before being arrested.

Nine days later, the protestors' numbers had grown to 150, and the police thought it prudent to call up reinforcements.

****

By April, the gymnasium, the university's disdain for the surrounding communities, and the SAS's increasing militancy were combining into a Molotov cocktail mix. Made more explosive by the issues surrounding the Vietnam War, and the aloof, generationally blind university president and trustees. Different modes of communication, different senses of propriety, and different goals and visions made a hash of the executive attempts to resolve any of the issues.

A simple inept protest brought the university to a panic stop.

Escalation

President Johnson and his advisors weren't the only ones who could intensify things. A small rally at the traditional Columbia gathering place, the sundial on Low Plaza, somehow morphed into a campus occupation lasting until it was broken by riot police six days later.

SDS (Students for a Democratic Society) and SAS had united for the sundial rally, but spontaneity, not planning, became the protest's hallmark. Little was planned but the original pieces opposing the gym. No one seemed to know what to do once those speeches were made. Yet there was enough malleable anger in the crowd to ensure something happened.

There was growing frustration the war seemed unstoppable, leaders blatantly lied, politicians said they didn't care how many people marched, and the anti-war movement was reviled by so many people. There was rage at the university's cooperation with the war industry and the Selective Service Administration. There was Black bitterness about those issues, but it was compounded by the racism they were surrounded by on campus, and in the conduct and effects of the war.

And of course, there was the gym.

*****

The joint rally suffered the plight of a ping-pong ball badly played, landing first here, then there, and nowhere near where the players wished. *Pling* to the sundial; *Plonk* to Low Library—oops there are jocks waiting; *Plick* to the gym site; *Plock* back to the sundial; *Plong* to Hamilton Hall.

At one point, marchers coming back *from* the gym site met more demonstrators headed *toward* the gym site.

Thus was Hamilton Hall, a small university classroom and administration building, occupied.

Inside Hamilton Hall

SAS and SDS could come together for a rally but found it hard to continue working together. The Black students were disciplined, united, and focused on simple goals, while SDS was attempting to radicalize the entire campus, and, in theory, to do it using a time-consuming participatory democracy process.

To an unaligned White sympathizer, the scene inside Hamilton was party-like and chaotic, making any serious purpose hard to discern. The night of April 23rd, SDS and other Whites—Tom Hayden, some faculty, community members, random groupies, and interested partisans—left Hamilton Hall. They left at the request of SAS, leaving the Black students, Black community members, and Black luminaries—H. Rap Brown, Stokely Carmichael, and Charles 37X Kenyatta—in charge of Hamilton's occupation.

I left early, before the mass White exodus. The mass went one way I went another. I wasn't committed enough to go to jail. However, a month later I would be anxious for a court date—but as a plaintiff.

One participant's account puts the White diaspora this way. *Over the next few days, the various mostly-White factions branched out to other buildings – SDS to Math, … the Trotskyites to Avery, the anarcho-syndicalists to Fayerweather, etc. (or something like that). In all, five buildings were occupied for a week.*

"Violence on a Harrowing Scale"
—*Cox Commission Report*

The night of April 29th began sultry, serene, and dreamlike. Buildings had been occupied since the twenty-third.

A row of city transit buses lined Low Plaza. Each one shouting from its colorful, backlit ad-boards *Butterflies Are Free!*

Each free butterfly bus was there to haul away arrested demonstrators.

Off-campus was a different story. The cops had been sitting in police transport on side streets for days, told they would be clearing Columbia buildings of protestors one moment, called off the next. Frustration and testosterone had to be climbing.

By early afternoon everyone paying attention had been informed the police would clear the buildings that night. They would not be called off again.

Columbia's decision to throw up her hands was one toke over the line to me, and I joined the human barricades forming at the building entrances. I had thought throughout the occupation, erroneously, that Columbia, with her experts in international diplomacy, would do better than resorting to force. No one outside the cloistered, aloof administration had any illusions the police would act with restraint.

Our living fence — an unsorted crew of professors, grad students, undergrads, hangers-on, photographers, radicals, tweeds, preppies, pukes, grubs, men, women, boys, and girls — had two goals. One remotely feasible. One not even remotely.

We were in front of the likely entrance-target at Low Library, the building SDS had taken subsequent to leaving Hamilton. It was conceivable, barely, that the mobilization of mostly non-radicals would give Columbia administrators an *AHA!* moment. Sudden understanding that they were crossing a line they didn't need to cross.

But it was not reasonable to hope our non-violent presence (and off-key singing of patriotic standards) would miraculously dissuade the police from entering the building, and instead send them home for a good night's rest.

I believe the outcome was known to both police officers and those of us facing them. The question actually was how violent would it be? The answer: more than needed, but we would see worse later.

I was somewhat casually tossed aside in the first wave, holding to passive resistance, and receiving only a few scratches and bruises from my hard landing on shrubs and concrete. The student next to me was not so lucky. His scalp was split open and bled copiously. The picture of him in his checked flannel shirt, dripping with blood yet defiantly flashing a victory sign, became an iconic image of the '60s.

Then, and only then, after the buildings were cleared, did the cops cry havoc and slip their demons. They ran wild, clearing and clubbing students from areas supposedly safe and trying to force them off campus—through tall wrought-iron gates irresponsibly, but stoutly, locked while the students piled up against them.

Knickerbocker Hospital's ambulances made more than twelve runs to the campus. Sixteen people got there on their own. Eighty-seven went to St. Luke's.

But nobody died.

What would have been the outcome of a police riot in one of the nearby Black and Brown neighborhoods? I'd learned enough through working in East Harlem, from following the civil rights struggles, and from viewing the riots in Watts, Cleveland, Newark, and New York to know the answer.

The Black caucus in Hamilton had better cards—and played them better—than did the White radicals. Achievable goals, simple process, and their cohesiveness made their endgame in Hamilton easier.

In contrast some of SDS's demands were labeled non-negotiable and seemed designed to back the administration into a lose-lose position. Give control of the university over to the students and faculty or call the cops.

Hamilton was the first building cleared. Black students had maintained contact with the administration throughout the week, and at the end of the week were in direct contact with the police. They also brought in legal counsel who stayed with them. Onlookers could not see their removal, because the police took them out through a steam tunnel, but the odds are it was an impressive show of solidarity and planning.

Gym Crow was never built.

Second Verse, Same as the First

Not only was I scarcely alone in making mistakes, I wasn't the only one making the same mistake twice. The bust on April 29th-30th left behind open metaphorical wounds as well as the half-mended physical wounds. On May 21st and 22nd SDS and President Kirk both yelled *Do-over!*

The issues between SDS and the administration shifted drastically in the weeks between the two crises. The gym was off the table, but disciplinary action against SDS leaders was very much in play. The result was exactly the same. An occupied building. Summoned police. Broken student heads.

****

Seven years later, the first time I talked to strangers about the bust on May 22nd, I was surprised by tears popping into my eyes, and I had to gather myself for a moment. That was awkward.

I was in front of a jury.

Only Hamilton was occupied in the second insurrection. Kirk called in the troops sooner this time. In the early morning police action — *after* they had already cleared Hamilton with no violence, plainclothesmen suddenly lost control and went rampaging over the campus south of Low Plaza. They began clubbing students on South Field, and when that fun was over, ran for Furnald Hall where they could see more students gathered outside the dormitory entrance.

When the students started to run back inside, the cops picked up speed, like a coyote running sheep. I was one of the last students to go out of the dorm, and one of the first ones back in. But I stopped in the foyer and held the inside door of the foyer open for the rest to hustle through. I began to perceive my chivalry might have been a mistake. By the time the last student was through the door, the cops were right there.

Some of the cops started beating me in the foyer while others pushed by to go inside. The ones smacking me dragged me out of the foyer, down the concrete stairs, and started beating me with disturbing pleasure and enthusiasm on the bumpy brick path outside.

Time slowed and I thought *Resist? Fight back? Curl up into a ball?* Curling up won, since some of my attackers had a perverse interest in my genitals. I can still hear the sound the billy clubs and blackjacks made on my head. Bizarre because you hear it inside your head and know it's your skull vibrating.

Turns out there were six of them waling on me, kicking, clubbing, sapping, groping, punching. My testicles were so frightened they retreated back inside. One guy brought a two-by-two into play. I think the two-by was what laid open my leg.

When they stopped — probably because they caught on the press was shooting film and a stretcher crew was heaving into view — the litter-bearers were already beside me, although I may have lost a moment

212

or two. A friend of mine held one shaft of the old army-style wood and canvas stretcher. That's all it took, a known friendly face, and the tears came. The friend seemed shocked. I sucked the tears back in.

While I was being beaten by the cops and subsequently jounced by student volunteers over to St. Luke's for stitches and bandages, the rest of the cops were ransacking Furnald. They went beating their way through students as far up as the fourth floor before sanity, or the recognition of what they had done, turned them around.

****

Some of the plainclothesmen hadn't waited till I was out of their way to get into the dorm. They went in through the windows. Inside it was blood-lust frenzy. Enough with the smarty-ass kids and their freaking causes. They found the spokesman for SDS and used him for bat practice.

When I met him two days later, he still looked like shit. Swollen eyes, lumpy face, drooping split lip, purple-yellow bruises. Stitches here and there. He pretty much said the same about me.

But he said it with a tone of horror I can't muster, because he was witness to the ferocity of their start on me. I was spared seeing it happen to him.

****

His name was Ron Carver, and he and I were the only ones of the scores of beaten and traumatized students who took legal action. I thought there would be dozens like us. We met for the first time in the law offices of David Drexler, an American Civil Liberties Union member who was willing to take our cases on contingency. He had been revulsed and outraged by what happened to us.

213

We were glad to make his acquaintance.

****

It took much longer than we expected for the case to come to trial. By 1975, both Ron and I had left the city. He was organizing labor in a factory, but still in the Northeast, while I was working as the hired man on a gentleman's hobby farm in the rural West.

My tears came as our trial lawyer—David didn't do the trial work, only the prep—walked me through my story. When we got to the beating itself, I lost it for a moment. I'm pretty good at burying emotions away, yet sometimes they'll pop out and surprise me.

Yet the city's trial lawyer was the one who was most surprised.

****

Not by the tears. Once I got myself together, we introduced photographs he should have known were coming. He knew about the grisly ones of Ron and me post-beatings. But the pictures we had from the press were a revelation. His prep attorney had done the kind of due diligence that gave government hacks their bad name. When the trial guy saw pictures he didn't know about, he immediately asked the judge for a conference.

Ron and I wondered while the two attorneys met. When ours came out of the conference room he walked us a short way down the hall into a different room and announced *We have an offer to settle*. Ron, who had been much more seriously damaged than I, would receive seven thousand 1975 dollars. I would get three thousand.

The jury appeared favorable for us, but Ron had been much more involved in the radical actions on campus than I had, and his testimony and cross examination were yet to come. He also got word his factory's

214

management was beginning to suspect he was more than a laborer. And was searching for a reason to fire him. He needed to get back on the job.

Our attorney recommended accepting the offer. We agreed.

Everybody went back to the courtroom. The judge made an announcement of the settlement and thanked the jury for their time. And the trial was over. We had won! (Technically a settlement in our favor, but to us—we won.) The attorneys shook hands and the city guy whispered something to our guy, and they separated.

****

It was the public photos. True, in the proof-of-injury snaps Ron and I looked like extras from a zombie apocalypse movie, but it was the press photos that mattered.

My picture had been splashed over page one and page two of the New York City Post. Page one had two pics: one showed six guys beating me, the two-by-two in evidence; the other showed me being carried off the field of riot, a plainclothesman gazing down at me. The city was planning to argue we had no proof these were actually cops. *Probably street hooligans.* The city's prep guy didn't manage to get the photos into their file.

The rest of the film-roll which didn't get published? Worse for the cops. But the press photos made them unnecessary. The plainclothesman admiring his handiwork? His badge is clearly visible in the page one photo, inside his flopped-open coat and pinned upside down. To make the number harder to read.

****

Our trial lawyer treated us to lunch. He wanted to know if we were more seriously damaged than the settlement reflected. We thought not.

215

We had lost our political point in the first round. Despite our belief President Kirk knew what would happen when he telephoned for New York's finest the second time, the judge ruled Columbia could not be held liable and severed the university from the cases. Ron and I had been disappointed, but not surprised, and were content with the settlement.

Our attorney made our day still better by saying *The city attorney said, and I quote, "I nearly shat my pants when I saw that photo of the cops."*

In Passing

Kelley died that year.

I let it go by, hardly noting it. For years he was my refuge, and I let his death go by. Doing so seems wrong now. My pitiful excuse is that I couldn't afford to mark his death. Psychically I couldn't deal with it then.

But I've got a pattern with death. Like Scarlett O'Hara *I'll think about that tomorrow.*

There's a toll that comes with it.

That Summer of '68

I let Kelley's memory and the Y's Director, Pop (and myself), down that summer. The cops' saps, billy clubs, and random wooden posts seemed to have knocked out my moral compass. Almost a funhouse mirror reflection of what Merle wanted to do with baseball bats to Black noggins.

Despite my knowledge of the Good Thought Notebook, I, in short order:

Put a ding into Camp Pine Tops brand-new pickup;

Denied that I had done so;

Got caught storing a rubber in my wallet,

216

By kids to whom I was supposed to model appropriate Y-type behavior;

And made a hash out of my summer job assisting Kelley's replacement at Pine Tops.

***

I have no defense for the summer, but it brings back an unsettling memory of Kelley.

When Stan and Roy and I were running around together as kids, Roy was the first one of us to start cursing. When that first *Damn!* Popped out of Roy's mouth I was so shocked I ran home. Cursing had been such a big deal for some of us church going, Y-going, little upright citizens, *Damn!* drove me right out of Roy's house when he let the word fly.

****

It ate on me. I didn't want to get my friend into trouble, but I was worried about him, and worried about what I should do. There was supposed to be some kind of punishment coming for cursing. God didn't like cursing. Or was it OK and merely something pronounced by grown-ups to make us fit their mold of a good person? I didn't know.

****

The conundrum was enough to put me off my feed, feel queasy, and knot my stomach. Maybe Kelley noticed and that's why he invited Roy, and Stan, and me out to Pine Tops for a weekend.

He said he had a chore for us, and he did. A bigger than one-boy job. Spring was coming and it was time to get the Pine Tops pool cleaned out. It was mainly drained, but over the winter branches and leaves and rain had fallen in and clogged the drain. Our job was to get the branches and leaves out and sweep the remaining water over to the drain.

It wasn't too big a task, but it was big enough we were proud to do it. Working for Kelley it was easy to forget my uneasiness and work with Roy and Stan like nothing was the matter.

Plus, when we got down to the last corner in the deep end and started throwing the branches and leaves out of the pool—in the deep end sometimes it took the three of us to get stuff out—we found the biggest, ugliest bullfrog we'd ever seen.

Stan ran to get Kelley. He'd like to see it. And Roy and I hovered around the big guy, acting like we were still working, but mainly watching the glumpy big frog, knowing we shouldn't poke at him, but wanting to.

Stan came back with Kelley, who agreed we were seeing one big, ugly frog. Kelley stayed there watching while we caught him. It wasn't easy. Ten-twelve feet at a hop made it so we didn't catch Big-Ugly till we herded him into a corner. Trapped, he tried to hop straight up the vertical walls to get away from us. It was his downfall. Literally. We caught him when he fell back.

And jointly carried him to a much better home in the brushy drainage ditch beside the pool.

****

After the excitement was over, Kelley asked me to come with him and help get lunch together while Roy and Stan collected the last of the little stuff in the pool. I figured Kelley knew something was on my mind and wanted to give me a chance to talk about it.

I went with Kelley, and by the time we'd walked up the granite outcrop between the bunkhouse and the chapel I'd squeezed up enough courage to ask him my question.

Kelley, I don't know what to do. Roy said a curse word. We were over at his house and we messed something up, and he said "Damn." And I don't want to get him in trouble, but what should I do?

I knew Kelley could make this right. He could tell me something simple and true and my world would square up again. I knew this.

But it didn't happen. We walked on in silence. On over and down to the cookhouse. And the silence hung between us.

15. School's Out

The Jim Weddell Rule

I graduated. Barely.

Barely because I was blind to the further disintegration which would possess me if I didn't get out of Columbia successfully, and therefore blind to the need for checking to make sure I had met the requirements. Since I hadn't seen an advisor for a long time (usually I scribbled his signature on my registration card) nobody had warned me of the dangers I was running.

I was one credit shy of meeting graduation requirements and didn't have enough credits of the proper level for any known major. Plus, I was so mentally disorganized I hadn't seen it coming.

But the administration changed their mind about PE. It would no longer be required after freshman year, and, seemingly just for me, they applied the rule retroactively. It could have been the Jim Weddell Rule. I had plenty of PE credits and they easily took up my one-credit deficit.

So now I was merely a major short of getting out. I had enough credits for a minor in English and for one in Sociology, but not enough in either one for a major. This time they turned a blind eye; and I was done.

I've always thought they had such a bad time with our class they didn't want any of us hanging around any longer.

Close Quarters

After graduation, I chose to stay in New York. I didn't know what I was going to do, but I wasn't going home.

A friend told me about a summer job opening, a traveling summer camp for kids from Long Island, and I grabbed it. It took care of my immediate needs—food, shelter, and some cash—and I could put off actual decisions for another two months.

I drove a new Ford Club Wagon van pulling a tent trailer to California and back. Sole driver and camp counselor for seven thirteen-year-old boys, including one secret bedwetter. Eight of us slept in the tent trailer. In one town I snuck away, washed and dried the bedwetter's sleeping bag, and managed to keep his secret. I did it for his morale, but the air quality did improve, slightly, in our overcrowded trailer.

Ten thousand miles later, when we got back, I found my girlfriend (I had discovered a way to meet girls finally) was living with another guy.

That was a relief. My guilt from out-of-wedlock sex was strong enough to keep me with her, and to ask her to marry me, but it was a mistake. She may have recognized the problem before I acknowledged it.

****

So there I was, back in New York with cash in my pocket but not a job, a girl, or much of a direction known. I crashed with some friends, found odd jobs, and shortly returned to work for the city's Addiction Services Agency, the outfit I had worked for in East Harlem.

Sheepshead Bay

The longstanding Italian restaurant held a single, carefully crafted stained-glass window. In deep hues, dignified, subdued, and a little out-of-place. The theme was maritime. As I remember it today, the simple engraved brass plate said only

In memory of Dominic, beloved brother,

lost at sea - 1928

According to Vera, our secretary old enough to have known the brothers, Dominic was blown out of the water by the Coast Guard while he was running liquor in from Canada. The date was correct.

Welcome to Sheepshead Bay, Brooklyn. Lesser-known neighbor to Coney Island and its amusement park and boardwalk. But perhaps as colorful in a different way.

****

Never-ever willingly accept an assignment pitching a social program to armed Brooklyn cops coming off shift. They want to go home. And you're in their way.

It is a dicey proposition.

****

In 1969 my message was particularly unwelcome. It was a plea to divert teenagers busted for small amounts of weed into our fledgling youth center. *Youth center* was a euphemism. Our ASA team was opening the agency's first drug program specifically for teenagers.

I was told the nascent center was a direct result of political pressure from the White middle-class community. Implied was that a lot of eyes were on us. Also implied was that this was to be the first ASA center in a White residential neighborhood.

Turned out I was not well-qualified for the job.

****

I was happy to have a job, but not particularly happy to be back with ASA. I was driven by my need for a better income, and at least I knew something about the agency. On paper I was more than qualified. In addition to my previous ASA work in East Harlem, I had worked with kids on and off since junior high.

Yet it wasn't enough. Spending a week living in a therapeutic community run by ex-addicts and another week being trained as a community organizer, wasn't the same as being shown what I would be doing in the youth center and how other people did it.

The problem for ASA was I was pick-of-the-litter as far as they were concerned. The community organizer said I was his best trainee. ASA needed to open the center in a hurry, and, to me, the other new hires seemed, if possible, less sure of what was going on than I was.

My new boss, Jean, was only occasionally clear about what I was to do, and never about how to accomplish it. She seemed to think our staff en-counter groups—quasi therapy and emotional outlet sessions—would solve any problems, that I had more experience in these groups than I possessed, and that there was no need to lay out the framework of how the center would operate, what it would offer the kids, and how we could facilitate change.

****

The community organizing training had been good, but not what I needed. However, it left me with a moment I will always treasure.

We were winding down the encounter group which would end our second week of training. There had been some difficult moments in the group and some moving ones. One tough, street-wise, clean junkie had let her guard down enough to talk about her need for a better job.

224

Because of her background, she was almost unemployable for anything other than addiction counseling.

What about domestic work? I offered.

Maiding? she bellowed. *Are you telling me about maiding? My mother done enough maiding to last me my whole life!*

I probably paled. This kind of explosion was what encounter groups were about. I rarely responded well. I could muster nothing but a feeble, *I'm sorry.*

Don't take his head off, he's only trying to help. Some of the rest of the group jumped in. But she was right to confront me. I was sincere but sincerity wasn't enough. She needed knowledgeable help.

At the end of the group, she startled me. She came over. *You mean it, don't you.* A statement not a question. *Yeah, I do.* (Some people in encounter groups put on an act. It most often fails.)

I didn't need to go into my backstory. We could hear each other's accent. She knew the attitudes I had had to unlearn, and what I had yet to learn. And I knew some of how Whites had treated her and her family.

I basked in a rare moment of mutual acceptance and appreciation.

****

Bernice and I shared a warming hug, and when we separated, I was uncharacteristically and ill-advisedly emboldened, *Can I touch your hair?* Bernice wore a beautiful afro. She looked at me quizzically, thought about it, and agreed.

But added—with a smile, *What is it with you White guys and our hair?*

****

For both those short conversations I thank Willie and Wilucia, who showed me enough to make me understand I could do things without question they could only dream of doing.

And I thank East Harlem—where the housing project elevators smelled like piss; the fourth floor walkup hallways smelled worse and added broken windows, peeling paint, and burned-out lightbulbs to the mix; where the White police wouldn't come; the White landlords didn't care; and the Black and Brown people treated kindly a naïve cracker-sounding White kid—a neighborhood that profoundly altered my understanding of the world.

Misfits

Big Y summer camp kids were light-years away from urban misfits in Brooklyn.

The Sheepshead Bay teenagers liked me, but liking didn't quite cut it. We were supposed to do more than make them fond of us. We were to steer them away from drugs, help them and their families examine their family dynamics, and see what changes might work for the better. Our mantra was *Drugs are not the problem. Drugs are only the symptom.*

I still believe the mantra, but it was a tough sell to parents who wanted to blame the kids or the drugs, and not themselves.

I was not comfortable in the job, and my manager Jean had her own insecurities about her role as boss. She planned a camping trip for staff and clients, got sick the night before, yet sent us out anyway. No prep, no planned activities, no rules, no instruction, no watch-duty. The teenagers—testing limits—snuck in liquor, and, while the staff slept, boys and girls visited each other's tents and had a party.

The weight fell on the staff. The following two days of corrective actions—confrontations, staff meetings, talks with parents, an encounter group with the kids, confrontations with each of the ringleaders by themselves—were learning days for me, but my relationship with Jean never went anywhere but downhill. I lost what little self-confidence I had from the training sessions, and Jean became so frustrated with me she ordered me to her office for a come-to-Jesus meeting.

She had only one complaint, but it was global.

According to her, *You have so little sense of self that I can't tell who you are, and I can't work with you.* The only way I could save my job was if I went into counseling.

****

Jean was specific about the counseling, which was good. Because I was mentally out for the count.

Her direction was simple and clear. The only time I heard such from her.

Go to Group Labs. They run therapeutic encounter groups under the direction of a psychiatrist. Ask for an intake interview, and sign-up for weekly group sessions. They will explain the process. Here's their address and phone number.

Your choice is do that or be fired.

I was confounded. I knew I was in bad shape, but I didn't think it showed so much. I wanted to fight back, but I didn't have the oomph. Those cans I had been kicking down the road finally landed together and created a rattly, treacherous mountain I couldn't climb. While I didn't agree with her *no sense of self* stuff, I didn't think she was belittling me. I sensed deep down she might be throwing me a life-preserver.

I grabbed it.

Boy Meets Girl

A slim woman detached herself from a chattering clique and made her way to me. Blonde hair gone pale-oak met a face made for photographs. Blue eyes so strong, black-and-white would catch the color. I didn't know her.

Our group's going out for Chinese. Would you like to join us?

I would. I was together enough not to waffle or turn down the nicest offer that had come to me in months. *It sounds lovely.* I didn't add *Like you.* But I should have.

The clique was the remainder of her encounter group. The members who still were amiable. Who hadn't fled as quickly as they could. Amiable wasn't always your emotional state at the end of a group therapy session.

Sometimes you simply wanted to hide in a bed with the covers pulled over your head. Someplace safe.

That night, I was cleansed and open following my own group session. And I too had no particular place to go. Her name was Bertie, she introduced me around, and we left Group Labs' softly lit living room.

Oh Freedom!

They weren't *old* freedom songs then. They were simply freedom songs. Bertie, who came from a leftie family, and William, who was Black, started the singing. Five of us from the Chinese dinner were back at Bertie's place. Just hanging out.

I knew those songs too. Three ways. From singing the original gospel words, from hearing the civil rights/voting rights lyrics before I saw their light, and from belatedly joining in.

I happily sang with these previous strangers. Myself a long, long way

228

from home. Geographically and politically. My Georgia school district and my home church remained White-only (except for the help). One was unconstitutional, the other un-Christian.

We taught each other the songs as needed and everyone sang. They were a congenial, welcoming bunch (I sang poorly then) and their embrace was another marker, like Bernice's *You mean it, don't you*, in my transition from a racist heritage.

****

Bertie's luminous eyes were also a major part of my evening. They found their way to mine throughout the dinner and the after-party.

When she gave me her phone number as I left, my enchantment was complete.

Ratterman

Ratterman lived in my old apartment on the corner of 110th Street and Amsterdam Avenue. When I lived there, he and my former apartment-mate would enrich our hovel with microbursts of laughter, egging each other on to further and further bizarre continuations of tales best otherwise left untold.

Ratterman was a frequent flyer at St. Luke's Hospital, easy access across Amsterdam from Columbia and where the ER team stitched shut my police-battered skull. Ratterman didn't frequent the ER though. He checked in at the psych ward whenever his schizophrenia threatened to get out of control.

In a roundabout way, the psych ward is responsible for his winding up in the 110th Street digs. After graduation in '69 he needed another stay at the hospital. Thorazine, chloral hydrate (the ingredient for a

Mickey Finn knockout-drop), and counseling weren't holding the fort. The modern class of psychotropic drugs was a long way off.

While he was there, he met a young trumpet player from Julliard and fell in love. And she with him. But when Ratterman told his therapist he was getting married, the therapist pronounced, *Bob, you can't get married, you're a paranoid schizophrenic and you can't handle it. If you marry her, I won't see you again.* And he didn't.

Not my idea of a supportive therapist.

Ratterman and his horn player were married a few weeks later in the chapel on the Columbia campus, with a few friends happily, but worriedly, present.

The now united couple needed a bigger place than either one had. My airshaft apartment was the answer. I vacated it and moved up to the tenth and top floor in the same building, where other friends had a gorgeous, old-but-worn apartment in need of another inhabitant. And Bob and his soulmate moved into my previous lair.

Everything went smoothly while they settled in. Bob's friends breathed easier.

But I think we each held the same question, *What if the therapist was right?*

Caroline and Bill

My sister was living in Charleston, South Carolina, where her husband Bill had a job with the school district and she, for a change, was not in the paid workforce. She was expecting their first baby to arrive soon.

We telephoned occasionally—certainly more than I spoke with Mom—but the calls were expensive. Caroline also sometimes wrote or sent care packages. I was never a good correspondent.

Frequently Bill got on the phone and we shared some stories. His

Georgia roots were deeper and more rural than ours — by generations on the same land — yet he was rightly proud of having overcome the racial limitations of his birthright.

Sometimes, however, there were bumps in the road out.

He told me, *I thought I was up to speed on racial issues, and ahead of many of my White co-workers. Then one of my Black friends at the School District pulled me aside and whispered to me, "Bill, it's Negro not nigra."*

Bill was mortified of course. But back home for him, in the White society of Cherokee County, using *nigra* instead of the N-word in the '70s made you sound like a hated race-mixer.

16. Grace Incognito

From the Christian tradition of my childhood these words echo—Justi-fication by Faith through Grace. What they mean is a mystery.

Yet a piece of the concept remains in my heart. *You can't earn Grace, but if it happens to you it's a blessing.* A Unitarian-Universalist minister, Munro Sickafoose, put it this way, *Grace frequently appears as those seemingly random moments that call us to something larger.* I would add, *"or save us from something worse."*

First Date

Before Bertie, it had seemed like a long dry spell since my previous girl-friend dumped me. I didn't handle it well.

Desperate and needy, I saw myself becoming the very model of a modern major loser sending out waves of sad, pitiful anti-pheromones. And yet my instinct was to run away from Bertie. I couldn't stop working against myself. I lost her number two or three times. Waffled in vague ambiguities. Got lost in my own head.

And then she took the initiative.

She invited me over to dinner at her place. Relieved, I accepted.

The day of the dinner started horribly.

Ratterman's Last Flight

Ratterman committed suicide in the wee morning hours. He jumped off our roof, most likely passing by my window as I slept. It was, and is, a sad and disturbing thought. But stunned and grieving as I was, I didn't break the date with Bertie, or seek support.

When I got to Bertie's place on West 94th I had a surprise. It was a dump. I had been so taken with her I hadn't noticed.

The neighborhood was sketchy, abandoned cars and winos abounded, and the neighboring building was an SRO — single room occupancy — hotel, which meant it was a low-rent dive, filled with screaming, punctuated by crashing bottles.

Her apartment itself was cramped, harshly lit, and every room opened from one narrow linear hallway. The whole place smelled a little off, because of the neighborhood — and because of the resident squirrel monkey, her roommate's pet.

The night was doomed from the start because I didn't, and wouldn't for a while, tell her about Ratterman. Group Labs hadn't worked its *be open and acknowledge your feelings* magic yet. I was still an emotional stone. Inwardly I was a cauldron. Externally, not a ripple in the surface.

Home-Cooked Meals

Another surprise. Bertie's cooking was different. Mom's cooking wasn't good, but it was plain. I grew up on standard Southern fare, fry everything not a vegetable, and some of those, too. Boil everything left desperately, preferably with fatback, bacon, or some other dead pig product. White bread, ketchup, and baloney sandwiches are a solid lunch. In fact, you don't need the baloney.

So, I am not a foodie. Bertie served me spaghetti. A nice dinner—scratch-made red sauce, green spaghetti, simple salad.

I was intimidated.

I knew the spaghetti wasn't green from mold, and recognized its intention to be glamorous, but Mom's recipe for spaghetti involved ground meat, ketchup, and spaghetti—regular old white spaghetti.

That's all.

I swear Mom threw the spaghetti straight from the box into the hamburger/ketchup mix in the frypan and simmered everything together. (Caroline says *No, she did cook the spaghetti first!*) Anyway, I loved it. I don't say those words often about her food.

And I panic at the sight of new food. The expectations are too high, and the risk of offense too great. I failed at both. You can't hide it, when you're pushing food around the plate and taking tiny bites.

It's for You!

Fate wasn't done making a hash of Bertie's attempt to jump start our sputtering relationship. Her telephone rang. It was for me.

Caroline calling *You've got a niece!*

So I spent half an hour not eating and spent another half-hour talking to my family. Bertie didn't kick me out, which was kind, to say the least.

We chatted for a while in the living room after dinner, but I was bad company. Ratterman was dead. I'd made a fool of myself with my picky eating and poor manners, and my sister had a new baby. Though Bertie wasn't throwing me out, even though I'd made such a hash of everything, it was all too, too much.

I needed to get away and hide, maybe cry. Retreat under covers.

I made wretched apologies and left.

Beneath my blanket I couldn't figure it out. I wept silently in close, dark frustration.

In those days I didn't have the capability to admit when I was angry. And that night, it seemed such a peculiarly wrong way to feel. I could feel it, but I couldn't name it or own it. But the unnamed feeling was focused on Bertie.

She put me in this situation.

But blaming her was so unjustified, so unfair. I could count the ways I had insulted Bertie, and she had been nothing but beautiful, pleasant, and interested. I couldn't be angry. That wasn't what I was feeling. I wasn't feeling anything.

I hadn't learned feelings aren't right or wrong, they're merely feelings.

Oh Sinner Man

I recovered somewhat, and after more wandering around inside my own head and finding nothing there, I squared myself away enough to find her number and call Bertie back. I thought I had a chance to make amends.

At Sheepshead Bay we were doing our own remodeling for the in-progress youth center. I thought demolition — tearing down walls, ripping out sheetrock, pounding out concrete — was more fun than rollercoasters. So, would she like to come and help?

She said no.

I didn't know what I'd done wrong, besides everything. But in my narrative, she had somehow gotten beyond my weird behavior. I thought she'd enjoy this off-beat outing. It appeared I was mistaken.

****

I thought I had asked *Would you like to come with me and beat down walls on our center?* Nothing wrong there in my mind. A little quirky maybe, but I expected there to be more conversation. When she turned me down flat I was flummoxed. My courage swirling away like hot sauce down a drain.

****

Years later I found out what she heard: *Would you like to come with me and help beat down walls on our sinner?* When she carefully enunciated this to me long after we left the city, I couldn't hear the difference. Finally, I got it ... *Beat down walls on our SINNER!* I could only assume — since she knew I was from Georgia and grew up in the church — that she thought it was some bizarre Southern religious rite like snake-handling. I too might have turned down a peculiar unknown ritual.

More years later, when the subject came up again, and I explained what I had conjured as her reason for the turn-down, she said *No, I just didn't understand, and I didn't want to ask.*

Southerners are, at best, careless with consonants and vowels. In our deepest dialects, outsiders need a translator. Somehow Bertie and I managed to dig our way out of this misunderstanding at the time, but without actually sorting it out for decades.

Possible only because she drove us around it.

****

We were never an obvious match. She was an exotic flower. An urban product of the city's public Hunter High School (for gifted girls) and the Midwest's University of Chicago. Beautiful in an elegant unforced way, her no-makeup approach was radically different from Athens' high school beauty queens. She was also not shy about her intelligence or

237

opinions. Culturally Jewish but not religious, she was raised in a big-C Communist family, in which her dad had chosen jail over pleasing the House Un-American Activities Committee.

I was nothing like that.

Against All Odds

Seventeen months later we were married. Twice. Once in City Hall to make it legal, again the next day on a beach at Fire Island to make it fun and to do it our way.

Sadly, I was in no way healed enough to invite Mom, who, the first time she met Bertie—knowing nothing about her except she might be Jewish—served her ham. Mom knew better. Bertie didn't care about the dietary rule, but I understood Mom was turning the knife. *She's not our kind.*

The next time Bertie and I were in Athens, the three of us ended up fighting. Bertie and I wound up shouting (not normally done in Mom's house), and Mom stormed out to go rejoin Dad. In a moment or two I went after her, as she knew I would.

But my refusal to invite Mom wasn't honestly about Bertie, it was about me wanting to be happy, and believing—with years of experience I thought backed it up—that Mom's nit-picking, fault-finding, projection of her needs onto others, and general manipulative personality would ruin the wedding for me—and for Bertie, and our friends.

****

Not inviting Mom meant not inviting Mary Win either. Mary Win loved weddings. Which tore at me. But not badly enough to make me behave better.

238

And Against the Flow

The crowd we were running with at the time, and Group Labs generally, was pretty liberal, pro women's rights, and slightly anti-marriage. There were lots of bad marriages, bad divorces, and several variations of *marriage is purely a property contract* sentiments—varying in heat like chili peppers.

A common question for us was, *Why do you want to do that?* Meaning get married. Bertie's mom even asked her. When they asked me in my therapy group, I surprised myself when I popped out with this, *Because it's an outward and visible sign of an inward and spiritual commitment.*

Their eyes did roll, and their jaws visibly dropped, and there were several pulses of dead silence. But it was possibly the most spontaneously honest words I'd ever uttered in the little lead-lined room—or anywhere else.

A Different Drummer

In the early days of our living together (and longer after than I care to admit) when I would go silent (often because I was hurt or angry), Bertie would march around me beating on pots and pans until I'd say something. A novel and surprisingly effective tactic, but something I hated. (Maybe because it worked.) More staggering is her seeing something in me worth fighting for so hard. Her arrival, persistence, and steadfastness were and are a definition of Grace. But not the first one I identified. Sometimes I'm slow to apprehend things.

Those beginning times with Bertie and my last months at Group Labs and Sheepshead Bay were formative. I regained much of the ground I lost when the mountain of cans I sent skittering down the road in my childhood and adolescence got their revenge. With pots and pans for background music, I learned to talk about what was going on with me, and finally, appreciate having someone to listen. But I'm still a work in progress, like a road under construction.

After Sheepshead Bay

I worked a variety of jobs after Sheepshead Bay—teacher's aide, taxi driver, handyman, elevator operator, office boy (upscale downtown law office, coat and tie for the office boy, a young secretary run off in tears for a pant-suit—skirts and dresses meant skirts and dresses *only*)—but in time I came back to addiction work.

I ran into Al again. He was introduced to me at a job interview. We recognized each other. He remained neat, compact, bald, and Black. I persisted White, but I'd lost the big hair, the black leather jacket, and the motorcycle didn't come with me for the interview. He recognized me anyway.

Al was working the streets, the cop-shops, and the courts rounding up clients for the non-profit considering hiring me. The organization was struggling to transition from a wealthy woman's charity group into a functioning training program for ex-junkies.

They offered me the job. The neighborhood in the South Bronx was rough, and the elevated subway a dubious ride. But I took it.

****

We trained ex-addicts in the building trades. From framing to flooring. The trainer, Ron, was gifted in science and engineering, with an enormous number of skills, and a master craftsman with his hands. But wildly disorganized.

I was hired because I had unusual credentials. Previous experience with addicts and addiction services, plus construction experience which included co-founding an apartment improvement business cited by *New York Magazine* as a *Best Bet*.

Building trades and ex-addicts were a good fit for me. I did know my way around construction, and I could see the enrollees as people not junkies, which was not always true of aspiring social workers in the field.

(A fellow social worker and I, a few years previous were to spend a week staying in a therapeutic community with recovering addicts as a part of our training. The setting was on an otherwise uninhabited island. My fellow trainee was horrified about living with addicts. I, in turn, was horrified by his fear. Who did he think the Addiction Services Agency was going to be dealing with?)

After a week on the job in the building trades program it was clear to me that I might not be the right person (too White and too young) to help Ron learn teaching is different from doing. It wasn't an explicit part of my duties, but it needed to be done.

I was hired to help the program get organized but making a list of required skills and a training sequence to impart them wasn't going to magically create order out of chaos. While I figured out a way to approach the challenge, I could earn my keep in other ways. Co-running an evening encounter group. Writing sections of grant applications.

And pushing a building permit through the corrupt NYC Building Department. You had to pay an *expediter* to run your application through the department. He was in actuality a bagman, taking some of your money himself and spreading the rest through the department. We refused to pay.

I have two versions of how it ended. One, I waited them out, showing up every day and asking *Where is our permit?* Hanging around and bothering people until they said *Come back tomorrow.* They caved.

Two, doing the hanging and bothering, but when it stretched out, *we* caved. (However, our mode of caving was to ignore them and construct the project without their permit.)

Through this, simply being around Al was inspirational.

The Crew

Ron—The crew-boss and trainer; a gregarious Black guy, mid-forties, strong build; could talk about books and cooking, explain multiple branches of engineering and physics, and rattle on about anything, it seemed. He repaired electronics for friends; knew how to demonstrate the math of carpentry and the correct way to lay down flooring adhesive. (Nice, big, sweeping arcs with the notched trowel.) But easily distracted.

Luiz—A thin, light-skinned, and blonde Puerto Rican. When a crew conversation veered towards jail-time and jailhouse sex came up, he volunteered *Yeah, of course I peddled my ass for smokes in jail. Everybody did it.* Opened my eyes a bit more.

Mike—I didn't know middle-class Black junkies/ex-junkies existed before I met Mike. He was solidly structured, in his mid-twenties, and handsome. At any chance he flirted with the female office staff. And showed up at my birthday party with two of them and a record they wanted to spin. Made my day. He liked to drive Corvettes, the redder the better. Gave racist cops an entirely new meaning for *jailbait*.

Raymond—The popular, stocky, muscular, normally quiet Black cook. But don't mess-up his kitchen. He and the crew built it.

At the 1971 New Year's office party in the project multi-purpose room, I asked Raymond if I could use his kitchen to heat my pot-luck dish. We spoke with similar accents but from opposite sides of the color line. A grudging *Yeah, but clean up your mess* was his curt response. I used one pot for the collard greens, and another pot for the black-eyed peas and ham-hocks. The smell drifted out into the lunchroom. Raymond drifted back in. He watched me stirring for a while. I got nervous. Raymond leaned in, sniffed deeply, and turned to me. *You eat that shit too?* I said, *Yeah I love it.*

Raymond studied me with new interest. Saw my wedding band. I seemed young. *You married?* I said *yes.*

What's her name?

Bertie, It's short for Bertha.

Raymond's final question, *She White?*

I say *Yeah, she is.*

Don't bother cleaning up, he offers, *I'll get it.*

Juan — Puerto Rican, with light brown skin. One of the steadiest trainees. Surprised me when he had beers with lunch. *It's customary on construction crews* he let me know. *Not where I come from,* I thought. But I didn't know the New York customs. However, I did know many drug programs made alcohol and drug abstinence *both* part of the deal. Ron was okay with it, and it wasn't my battle to fight. I had my hands full with what I was learning about the lack of progressive skill training and testing.

Reggie — A White union construction worker. Appeared mysteriously (to me) on the crew. Not an ex-junkie. I never did know why he was there or whose idea it was — maybe it was to increase efficiency? We had started using the crew as a money-maker (boarding-up abandoned buildings to keep the junkies from stealing the copper piping; a certain irony there). If he was a union carpenter, he was breaking union rules by working for non-union wages.

Izzy—A Black teenager, joined the crew after the other ex-dope-fiends, but before Reggie. Al sprung him from jail on probation: stay straight, in the program, and out of trouble. Izzy nicknamed me *Goggles*, for my big, squarish '70s eyewear, and drew a caricature to match. It caught on with the crew.

Izzy was re-arrested for street crime. For mugging someone—*taking them off*. He claimed innocence and staff wanted to believe. The crew was not so sure. Al was still making the hard calls. He visited Izzy in jail again. Talked with the arresting officers. Came back to the staff with *No, let him go, he's guilty.*

Everyone believed Al, but it was sad.

I wondered if it took Al back to when we first met.

Moon Shot

I traveled to work on trains I was advised not to take, walking to the IRT station at 96th and Broadway and catching the number two express train zig-zagging uptown and east. As prophesied, I was soon the only pale face in my car. When I transferred to the Third Avenue El, I was usually the only White person anywhere on the platform.

I was never hassled.

And by 161st Street, the cars were near-empty of any faces.

I chose to work my way up to the front car no matter where I entered the train on my El leg. There I could move through the cars to the very north end and peer through the door-window straight down at the tracks we were gobbling up. Or enjoy the track network magically extending further and further ahead. Carving a way between old-timey buildings.

Rarely, I joined somebody else enjoying the same view. Only once did another person join me. A kid in his early teens from his face. Open, enthusiastic. We talked about how exciting it was riding up front—like

244

choosing the first car of *The Cyclone* roller coaster at Coney Island. But also how cool it was to be up above the street watching third floor windows flit by.

We changed topics, right before my stop. It was NASA's heyday. Apollo 11 had landed the first two humans on the Moon in 1969. A string of manned missions followed. In 1971 everyday people were keeping up with Apollo 15's progress. Thirteen days total. Three of them on the moon. Eighteen and a half hours outside the lunar module. The contrast of the moon landing with both the aging 1870s elevated train infrastructure we rode, and the boarded-up, empty-lotted, fire- and drug-scarred community we traversed was inescapable.

The young man looked me in the eyes and said *You White folks are gonna just go and leave us right here. Aren't you?*

White Liberals

When I had occasion to drive a car through Harlem, I made it a point not to roll the windows up and lock the doors. To do so seemed like an insult to the neighborhood.

But I was once a passenger in the crew van, and half the crew was there. Mike was driving—even though the blue Dodge work vehicle was hardly a Corvette. The crew had insisted I ride shotgun, probably because my status was so ambiguous, they took the cautious approach and assumed I might be high-enough in the pecking order to warrant it.

We were riding south from the program offices to scope-out a new boarding-up job in Harlem, the first project outside the Bronx. As soon as we crossed over the Third Avenue Bridge and entered Harlem there was a flurry of activity inside the Dodge.

When I didn't join in Mike looked over at me like I was a doofus and said, *Roll up your window and lock the door.* "Idiot" was not uttered out loud.

Play Time

The playground south of our offices had a bad reputation. It was a miserable affair of asphalt, broken swings, bent-over basketball backboards with no hoops, and one little brick building.

Junkies lined-up in front of the building on seemingly random days to get a methadone fix. I was not a fan of methadone. It seemed an odd, and peculiarly American, way to deal with the drug problem. Give one drug to block the pleasurable effects of another drug.

But given the politics of drugs being sinful, it served its purpose. Though my ex-junkie friends told me, *Oh yeah. you can get high from it.*

On days that weren't methadone-days, the junkies hung out there anyway. Their friends came too. Thus, the playground's poor rep. When I chose to walk from 160th street to the number two train at 149th, skipping the ride on the El, I didn't like walking by it.

Nonetheless, I did it when I wanted the walk.

The predictable outcome? I had made it safely to the south end of the park at 157th Street when I heard a car stop, and these words.

Hey White boy, what cha doin' here? Hey honky!

And me? I was doing my *I'm cool* strut. Staring straight ahead, walking loose-jointed, No hurry. Sweating bullets.

Yo bro, what's your hurry? Come on, my man. Hey honky!

I crossed Third and I still wasn't turning around, but I heard the car slowly crawling along behind me. And I could feel their presence. There were at least three of them in the car and there was nobody around who appeared to be the rescuing type.

I said to myself, *I will not turn around and I will not run,* but I was not seeing a lot of good options.

Hey honky, what you got in your wallet?

My head turned without my willing it to. I knew it was bad.

And there were Raymond, Mike, Juan, and Luiz—in stitches.

246

Not Everybody Wanted to Play

My beloved bike was stolen off the street not long before Bertie and I first met at Group Labs. For years, I carried the serial number in my wallet and checked every R-50 *Bayersiche Motoren Werke* bike I could touch to see if it was mine.

Before the bike was ripped off, I would occasionally be dumb enough to run out of gas. To understand how dumb I was, it helps to know the fuel system had a manual reserve lever. When you first ran out of gas you could move the lever from the down position to the front position and access the reserve portion of the tank. Enough to take you miles further if the nearest filling station was far down the pike.

So, it was dumb, but there I was, pushing my bike to the gas station nearest me.

The filling station was one block east of Morningside Park and faced diagonally to the corner of 110th and Eighth Avenue, before the Frederick Douglass traffic circle went in. The station could get pull-in traffic from either street and sat on the southern edge of Harlem.

The location of this grubby filling station kitty-corner from the posh Central Park West neighborhood fascinated me.

Despite the corner's proximity to the *nice* neighborhood, Columbia students heard in freshman week, *Don't take the Number Two Broadway express subway past Ninety-Sixth Street.* Because its next stop is 110th and Eighth Avenue—right across from my filling station, and dangerously Black turf in the opinion of those doing the warning.

However, from where I was parked in front of my apartment building, it was but a short flat push east on 110th until I crossed Amsterdam. The station was a mere two blocks downhill from there. Once I got past Amsterdam, I could hop on the bike and let it coast to the station. Which trumped the perceived danger any day.

I glided into the station without a problem and hopped off the bike, putting it carefully on its stand (very carefully, since it outweighed me more than three to one), and pumped two bucks' worth into the tank. While I was pumping, an older model Cadillac pulled up to the pump next to me and the driver buzzed the window down.

Check the tires, the driver snapped. No, *Please*.

Unfazed, and happy to be mistaken for a working man, I asked, *How much you running?*

Thirty-two all around. The driver wasn't into pleasantries, only giving orders.

I kept a pencil-type tire gauge in my front pocket when I rode the bike, and from my cousins' garage in Michigan and my own kicking around I knew my way around a filling station. I thought I could have been content for a long time as a grease-monkey. But I wasn't often mistaken for one.

The driver's-side front tire was OK, and I moved around the car taking care with the hose so it didn't get trapped under a tire, doing the whole drill efficiently. Only the passenger front needed any air. I recoiled the air hose before I turned back to the Caddie.

The driver buzzed the window down again, asked me what I'd found, and I told him. *You were alright. Just a little low on the passenger side front.* He had an ear, because he asked where I was from. *Georgia*, I admitted.

Me, too, he echoed.

I lit up—I liked talking with fellow Southerners in the big city.

He didn't. At least not White ones.

He sneered, *How you like working for a nigger?* And buzzed the window up in my face before floating the big Caddy north onto Eighth Avenue.

The Conversation

Caroline and I were sitting in swings in a Michigan park. We faced each other with our swing-chains twisted up. In a little while we'd lift our feet and the chains would untwist. And we would twirl.

When we were kids, we'd take turns pushing each other, and after pushing and being pushed a couple of times, we'd each get a swing and pump ourselves *too high*. The destination every kid wants to reach. From going back and forth we'd go to doing the twisty till we got dizzy. Then we'd go home.

It was sweet to be sitting in swings side by side again and recalibrating our family memories. Mine almost always shine a harsh light on Mom. I always wondered why hers didn't. I didn't know she pondered the opposite question about me.

****

Jimmy, did Mom ever molest you? She was way out on our boundaries. But comfortable asking the question. We'd talked about Mom's propensity to walk around without clothes in the house, and how she always acted surprised if she should happen to startle somebody.

Should have been a straightforward *yes* or *no* question, if a bit unexpected. But her intuition was right.

****

Mom got squirrelly again when I was in junior high. It only happened once. I don't talk about it.

Everyone was home and the house dark and still. I was about asleep. The old trundle bed you're so fond of was lumpy and awkward, but it was nice having a settled place to sleep.

249

Caroline smiled, *You know why I'm so fond of it, right?*

Yeah, I do. I don't know how y'all managed it, but I know.

Sorry I interrupted, go on.

It's okay. So one night she comes out and surprises me in my drowse. We were both lucky I wasn't playing with myself.

"Are you awake, son, I couldn't sleep."

I told her I was awake. I didn't tell her it scared us when she couldn't sleep. We worried it would lead to something bad.

Caroline was surprised, *I didn't know you worried. I thought it was only me.* I told her I was continually amazed at how we lived in our own separate worlds in the same house most of the time. *Go on with your story,* she urged.

Mom whispered again, *"I know you're lonely out here by yourself. Come on in with me."*

There was a long pause on my part, but I said, "OK, Mom". Against better judgement. I enjoyed my alone time, when I was free to fantasize about anything I wanted to. You featured as an idea in one of them. I wished our society gave a boy one free introduction from his older sister.

Oh. I've wondered if you ever thought like that. I did.

I followed Mom into her bedroom. It was still unchanged from when Dad was alive. Their double bed on the far wall between the windows, her vanity with mirror and bench on the side wall nearest the door, and Dad's tall dresser next to it. Did you know he hid the bullets for the twenty-two in the dresser's top drawer?

No. How do you know?

When I was a little boy I used to sneak in there when no one was around, drag Mom's bench over, stand on it and play with the bullets. Once I took some out and hid them in her file cabinet hoping they would explode, and she'd be gone and we'd have Dad all to ourselves.

Truely? Caroline is mildly shocked. I walk it back.

Could have been a dream. I dream in color and it's a vivid memory.

250

Anyway, the night we were talking about, I followed her to her bed, knowing I shouldn't, but not able to do anything else.

I am so sorry, Jimmy. I should have been there.

There's a limit to what anyone can do, Sis. She should have gone and gotten you or Mary Win if she couldn't sleep. Why me?

She got in on the furniture side and I got in on the other. I crowded the edge of the bed, as far away from her as possible, and lay there like a corpse with my arms folded across my chest.

She said, as if she was doing something for me, "Isn't this better?"

I whined, Uhhh, telling myself she could interpret the noise however she wanted. I didn't want to lie to myself and her any more by saying yes.

I lay there in my cadaver pose, afraid to move. She breathed in. She breathed out. I matched my breathing to hers, making it as much as possible like I wasn't there. I had no idea whether she was awake or asleep, but her breathing was regular.

I wasn't drowsy anymore. Now I was awake. Awfully awake. Awake with my mind as closed as I could make it. It was too dangerous to open.

All I could do was match her breathing and count—In one, Out two, In three, Out four . . .

Did she do anything more?

Yeah, not much though. The ambiguity of it is what has made it so tough to talk about. It was inappropriate, but was it abuse? At some time, I almost fell asleep, but she rolled toward me and put her leg over mine. In the heat I slept in shorts; she slept in a slip. Her slip was up past her knees and I felt her warm thigh slide over my own. It was creepy-startling. She didn't seem to be awake. But I was.

My body tensed, and I went back to counting. In one, Out two, In three, Out four.

Jimmy, I'm so sorry.

Yeah, me too.

Hearing a Voice

Grace's place in my life struck me first in telling Mom's story.

I tried different ways of writing about Mom, my version of her life, but the way I liked best was fiction. I thought it was the only way I could distance myself enough to tell it.

In those versions, through an eccentric old lady's voice streaming into my head, I treated the reader to a stay in a 1950s mental ward and electroshock treatment. Mom's fictional roommate recounted her memories of Mom's experiences. How Mom endured electric current being forced through her brain, though it induced convulsions and caused memory losses. My garrulous character told how this went on for Mom every other day for a month straight.

But she continued.

Mrs. Weddell was worried about what would happen to the children. You do know about the children, don't you? It's why she was here. She had to get strong enough to take care of the children. They had no one else to take care of them. Only a neighbor lady and a faraway aunt.

I didn't know those words were in me, and I started to cry. Immediately morphing into sobbing—for Mom's pain and mine—and found myself forgiving Mom.

****

It was not until my fictional character spoke that I could see what it cost her to come back for us. It would have been easier for her to give up. To find a way to die or to retreat into full-blown insanity.

But she came back for us.

When my sobbing slowed and breathing returned to normal, I rewound my life-reel and played it again.

Realizing, *Grace, I think I've met you somewhere before.*

Acknowledgements

I am grateful to author and friend Hilde Lindemann who read and edited many drafts; my sister Caroline for her availability to rehash our natal family life together; all the friends and relations — Stuart Braman, Gretchen Stewart, Bill and Nancy Gruber, E. Kirsten Peters, Michele Sharpe (Michele Leavitt), and others — who saw pieces of the work-in-progress and were invariably supportive as well as clever in finding ways it could be improved. Thank you.

I appreciate Sayantani Dasgupta's invaluable professional assistance with all aspects of the process.

And special appreciation for my wife Bertie who, while involved in her own book's development, made space for this project in our lives and provided a sure and talented editing touch, and our children Wes and Angie for their support and good humor throughout this process.

The names of some individuals in Roadcuts Through the Heart have been changed, but all the characters and events are true as I remember them.

About the Author

Jim Weddell was born and raised in Athens, Georgia. After high school, he left the South for college in New York City. Work in social work and the building trades followed, but NYC was never home. In 1973 Jim and his wife moved to the rural West, where he found that architecture was a good fit for his interests in design, construction, and people. These led to a career in which Jim used his hands, heart, and head in the service of community development, historic preservation, and affordable housing.

Jim and his wife of 49 years live in eastern Washington, where he enjoys rafting, kayaking, biking, playing the banjo, writing, and being with friends and family.

CPSIA information can be obtained
at www.ICGtesting.com
Printed in the USA
FSHW010907060821
83663FS